**Proceedings of the 1977 Clinic
on Library Applications
of Data Processing:
Negotiating for Computer Services**

Papers presented at the
1977 Clinic on Library Applications
of Data Processing, April 24-27, 1977

Negotiating for Computer Services

J.L. DIVILBISS
Editor

University of Illinois
Graduate School of Library Science
Urbana-Champaign, Illinois

Clinic on Library Applications of Data Processing,
    University of Illinois, 1977.
    Negotiating for computer services.

    (Proceedings of the 1977 Clinic on Library Applications of Data Processing)
    Title on spine: Library applications of data processing.
    Includes index.
    1. Libraries — Automation — Congresses.
I. Divilbiss, J. L. II. Title. III. Title: Library applications of data processing.
IV. Series: Clinic on Library Applications of Data Processing.

Proceedings; 1977.
Z678.9.A1C5   1977   021'.0028'54s   [025.1'028'54]   78-13693

ISBN 0-87845-048-3

CONTENTS

INTRODUCTION

THE INCREASING USE OF automation in libraries has made many librarians painfully aware of the difficulty of negotiating for computer products and services. This is true for a wide range of situations, such as acquiring a turnkey system, joining a network, subscribing to an information retrieval service and many others. While negotiation should be a give-and-take process between parties on an equal footing, librarians often see themselves as being at a disadvantage. The product or service is technically complex, the legal instruments are mysterious, and the other party has greater experience with the technology, the law and the art of negotiating. The purpose of the 1977 clinic was to enable librarians to be stronger, more knowledgeable negotiators. Some of the papers printed here present negotiation from the librarian's viewpoint; other papers deal with the special needs and concerns of the vendor. In every case, the intent is to make negotiation a rational and orderly process. In their complementary papers, Boss and Gurr show that differing interests need not result in an adversary relationship between vendor and librarian. In his paper, Corey examines in some detail the special problems of negotiating when legally enforceable contracts are not possible. This paper includes several specific suggestions that prove extremely helpful for libraries that obtain data processing from a parent organization.

Three sessions of the clinic were devoted to explaining the basics of data processing contracts and conducting simulated negotiating sessions. The material used in the role-playing sessions is included here so that readers may practice negotiating in a risk-free setting.

J.L. DIVILBISS
Editor

RONALD W. BRADY
Vice-President for Administration
University of Illinois
Urbana-Champaign, Illinois

Negotiating for Computer Services: Must the Librarian Be Underdog?

NEGOTIATING FOR COMPUTER SERVICES is a subject that should not be all that controversial. After all, computer services in many forms have been used for a long time now. Further, I do not feel that the librarian must always be the underdog in negotiating for computer services. During the last several years, I have been involved in negotiating for computing services in various organizational arrangements at several different universities. These arrangements have included many different attempts to plan for, budget, manage, evaluate, upgrade and centralize/decentralize computing services, and each attempt had its own rationale. In reviewing the history of these different organizational strategies, it is clear that, although they are convincing individually, they do not form a cohesive group — and thus do not create an overall scheme for all users for all time.

In Illinois, the subject of computer services gained statewide concern in the mid-1970s, generating study and discussions. An outgrowth of this concern was an organization called the Illinois Educational Consortium for Computer Services (now the Illinois Educational Consortium), a not-for-profit corporation with membership composed of the systems of higher education in the state. It is an example of yet another form of organization dealing with computer services, and has its own set of problems.

Upon consideration of the many different forms of organizations and budgeting procedures, it becomes obvious that negotiating for computer services for libraries — or in fact for any large user — is a complicated process subject to a number of fairly technical discussions of the various components of computer services. Based on these considerations, the following discussion is a list of the major problems present in negotiating for large systems support — whether for libraries or other users. This list developed from discussion at similar conferences over the past several years involving data processing personnel, planners and administrative personnel.

First, there is a lack of communication among the technical people in computing service negotiations. For example, the initial problem is that communications will often begin between a person in a service organization and a person representing a large user such as a library. They typically start talking at each other, each in his own technical jargon. This situation seems to result in a failure of each party to understand the objectives. This is the most pervasive problem in negotiating; there is a lack of an understandable conceptual model on which to build. In time these two people might learn each other's jargon, but the constant evolution of terminology makes this a continuing problem.

The second problem is the lack of understanding by each party as to mutual commitments, such as editing, data entry, accuracy, special requests, maintenance, scheduling, etc. This is somewhat akin to the jargon problem mentioned above; and although this situation is probably not endemic to negotiations in higher education, such vagueness seems especially evident when trying to negotiate for such new systems. Discussion of technical details in the absence of an operational framework can result in serious misunderstandings. For example, one person might leave a meeting thinking that he understands what has been committed, only to discover two weeks later that his vice-president was either not committed to those things or was committed only to part of them. If such confusion can exist within an organization, the confusion resulting from negotiations between organizations can be crippling. Again, this lack of a good set of mutual commitments between two organizations results from the absence of a conceptual model. This predicament can be avoided if both a conceptual model and an operational model are formulated before any planned technical details are discussed.

The third problem I have noticed is a lack of adaptability on the part of either organization. Even a good systems analysis group within a good data processing organization will sometimes approach a problem unduly biased by previous successes. It is as if they were saying: "We have a well-tested solution; how can it fit your problem?" On the other hand, the library — or any other user, such as financial affairs, admissions and records, etc. — can also be guilty of rigidity. Each party has its own way of looking at the problem, which it believes to be not only relevant, but the *only* way to approach the situation. If each party approaches a supposedly mutual agreement with its own preconceived set of operational characteristics and jargon, and each does not commit the total problem to review, it is obvious why there are some bizarre negotiations.

The fourth problem is what I call self-serving analysis. I used to think — and probably still do to some extent — that by approaching a problem with an open mind and a willingness to devote the time required for a thorough investigation and analysis of the alternatives, a good cost-benefit model could be constructed, thus indicating the proper solution, whether it be submarine versus airplane or library automation versus some alternative. However, there are many possible judgments and interpretations involved, and there is difficulty in predicting the future. Some of the best systems have been realized because someone believed they could work, and in a sense made them happen. On the other hand, some systems that were well justified on a cost-benefit ratio became obsolete before they were completed. The wrong problem was being worked on, for the problem that was under design was the problem that existed — not the problem of the future. (The Department of Defense and the Army Corps of Engineers have shown that they can do the same thing, thus ending with an unsuitable weapons system or a misplaced dam.) Furthermore, there are several subpoints to consider under self-serving analysis: (1) marginal costing to attract the customer, (2) overstatement by the customer of cash substitution/replacement, and (3) overinfatuation with hardware by both sides.

In order to avoid becoming the underdog in negotiations, librarians must recognize the problem of marginal costing. Computer centers will often marginally cost a system in order to create a continuing need for new hardware. Moreover, in self-serving analysis, both parties have a tendency to overstate the substitution of cash for the new system. In my experience, very few computer systems installed in the educational environment have reduced cost, although they may have improved service. This is true even though many systems were sold or offered on the basis that implementing the system would result in savings of people and operating costs. The alternatives should have been analyzed or presented on other bases, including considerations of better services, long-term savings rather than short-term savings, etc.

The third part of self-serving analysis is infatuation with hardware. Often those who request data processing services and those who provide the service will tend to design a system around a piece of hardware, which necessitates developing a system to suit the hardware. It is rarely possible to dissociate oneself from existing hardware sufficiently to design a system and then find the hardware to produce it. One example of such a system, however, is the PLATO computer-aided instruction system that was designed and literally built here at the Urbana-Champaign campus. The specifications for that computer system were described before the appropriate hardware existed, and the hardware was subsequently invented.

The fifth problem is the unintelligible budget; this is probably a familiar concept, and many participants at this clinic may even be good at constructing one. It is part of the self-serving analysis, but should be considered as a separate component in view of the confusion it can add to an already ambiguous situation in trying to determine commitments for resources. Consider one element of the unintelligible budget: "funny money." The term means, among other things, money that can be spent only for a specific purpose. Marginal cost accounting is another budget problem. It involves budget projections based on estimated costs per fiscal year. Often, budgets for new systems are prepared in the spring — seemingly making for less cost. This type of budgeting, however, creates piecemeal programs — a third part of the unintelligible budget. It is certainly not in anyone's best interest to have vague understandings, funny money, incomprehensible budgets, etc. The necessity of dealing with general assemblies makes analytical and complete plans — with all commitments and no funny money — seemingly impossible. Thus, long-range commitments are difficult, and budgets are established which cover perhaps only one-third the cost for the immediate future.

The final problem concerns the arguments among the technicians. This often turns into an entire series of subarguments. There are three points to be made in this regard. A familiar controversy concerns the merits of the minisystem or the stand-alone system versus those of the large consolidated center. Arguments about this are often the self-serving arguments of techicians and not necessarily based on the realities of the hardware or support system. A second controversial point is the software — whether it should be "home-grown" or purchased. There are few examples of successful transplants of rather large systems from one place to another. (One such example, however, may be the University of Illinois's use of the library system developed at Ohio State.) This argument about home-grown versus purchased software is one of the factors impeding successful negotiation. Finally, there is the definition of "the system" — a term which has been overused. But what can be substituted for it — "the campus," "the university," "the state," "the world"? It isn't just a problem of library systems, but of financial and other systems as well. Discussion of the system at any level always involves discussion of size. Consider consolidation in terms of economy: if consolidation occurs at the campus level, for example, that is economy; if it occurs at a higher level, that is diseconomy. Each "system" feels that way.

Following are a few suggestions for negotiating. All things considered, I do not think librarians need be the "underdog" in negotiation. Historically, users of a consolidated or centralized facility have been the underdog to some extent, but for reasons given earlier, the two negotiating parties ought to be on equal terms.

Each side should try from the beginning to avoid the philosophic argument over central services versus autonomy and to examine with an open mind the alternatives in terms of the conceptual model. There may be models which have not yet been tried, such as branch computer centers. Such a center might resemble a branch library in that it would be self-contained for hardware and software, and maintain a management relationship to the central organization as an item of its budget. Both sides should concur that the purpose is not to debate autonomy versus centralization, but to construct a conceptual model of needs and to explore alternatives. For instance, economies of so-called minicomputer systems are much better than people realize. Many people — particularly in the data processing world — don't want to investigate them. Thus, negotiation should begin not with philosophic argument but with a conceptual model.

Second, new relations between libraries and computer centers should be considered. Both parties, however, should be aware of the pitfall of protecting self-interests and should seek to avoid it.

A third suggestion is to discuss issues at the policy level before the proposals become technical in nature. The central importance of a library to a university, for example, mandates an understanding on the part of the highest level of the administration of the technology of libraries and its possibilities, the library's budget, etc. — and to have a grasp on the future implications as well as the present status of these aspects. It would be helpful to obtain policy understanding, i.e., an agreed-upon set of conceptual objectives, before entering into negotiation for technical systems.

Fourth, it is in the best interests of both the user and the supplier of data processing services to prepare realistic budgets and time limits. One of the most consistent and long-term problems has been the attempt to do all or some of the things described above (e.g., oversell, underestimate cost, underestimate time frame, or overestimate substitutions) in the name of profit. The result is disenchantment, disillusionment and a desire to give up. There may be a trend among presidents, deans and top administrators in higher education today to understand and accept a slower growth curve of new activity, whether for library support systems or academic programs. Today, many new situations limit the growth we had come to regard as normal. This is not necessarily negative, but may encourage a growing "businesslike" attitude in terms of greater constraint, systematic approach, longer-term outlook, and less overstatement. Therefore, preparation of realistic budgets and time frames is important to both organizations.

Finally, the concept of an internally developed contract is important because it supports all of the above objectives. It will minimize problems outlined here and can be a means of incorporating some of these suggestions into acutal negotiations. A contract should result from a conceptual model, an operational model and a full budget incorporating everything in an understandable and readable manner. With such a contract, the administration of each party can determine what is to be delivered and when it is to be delivered on the basis of stated budget projections, costs and services required. Such a process will help to ensure each party's satisfaction from the agreement.

In conclusion, it should be remembered that the librarian (or any customer) should not consider himself the underdog in negotiations, nor should he believe that a group of systems analysts can define needs, or that the appearance of a new piece of hardware or software demands its immediate acquisition. Instead, librarians should continue to monitor and evolve needs, with a view to the future as well as to the present. Consideration of these needs from the viewpoint of others, e.g., the computer center, the budget, the state, should also be given. There is no reason to be intimidated — but each party should remember to get the full plan approved.

GLYN T. EVANS
Director of Library Services
State University of New York
Central Administration
Albany, New York

Regional Network Contracts with Libraries for OCLC Services

THIS PAPER IS WRITTEN solely from the viewpoint of providing OCLC services; therefore, unlike the other papers in this clinic, it is barely concerned with the act, or perhaps art, of negotiation. Rather, it deals with the complexities of the fiscal and administrative environment in which regional library networks and their member libraries exist, and the problems of developing a service contract within this environment. Negotiation, in the competitive sense, is seldom a factor here. The library wants the service and the network can provide it; how can it best be done? Before examining the regional network and library contracts, however, the structure of the Ohio College Library Center (OCLC) network should be described.

Structure of the OCLC Network

Following the initiation of the on-line services at OCLC in August 1971, a number of regional library consortia requested that OCLC provide services to their regions. OCLC's agreement to do this led to the massive service now provided. The first regions to contract with OCLC were Cooperative College Library Center in Atlanta, New England Library and Information Network (NELINET), Union Library Catalog of Pennsylvania (which subsequently became PALINET), Pittsburgh Regional Library Center, and Five Associated University Libraries (FAUL) in upstate New York. As of April 1977, 19 regional networks have contracts with OCLC; the system has grown to 1553 terminals and 1182 libraries, and projected growth for the next year will bring the totals to 1850 terminals and 1300 libraries.

OCLC's organizational structure is outlined in Figure 1. OCLC has service contracts with two types of groups. Individual participants have direct contracts with OCLC. This group includes members in Ohio, and libraries which were in geographic areas not covered by regional consortia (although a consortium may be established later, e.g., the Western Service Center in California, through which OCLC provides "regional" services to direct participants). Regional networks account for approximately 87 percent of OCLC's terminals. "Other networks" account for other services for which a network may contract, e.g., BALLOTS, Bibliographic Retrieval Services, and for which OCLC may at some time also contract.

The regional network has a contract with a user. For purposes of this discussion, *user* is defined as a library or institution with a contract for OCLC services with a network, in which a terminal (or terminals) is housed on the premises of the contracting institution. Finally, in some cases, a group of small libraries has agreed to "share" a terminal housed in one of its institutions. Such agreements are usually embodied in a separate contract or letter of agreement among the sharing libraries.

The regional networks also have their own individual structure. Some are multistate consortia, such as NELINET, SOLINET and Amigos. They may have a formal relationship with a regional educational consortium; for example, NELINET is part of the New England Board of Higher Education. Some networks are state agencies, such as INCOLSA in Indiana; in other cases, network services are provided by state agencies to libraries in the state, e.g., State University of New York (SUNY), and ILLINET in Illinois. There are relatively small consortia contained within one state (such as FAUL and PRLC) or centered in one city, as is CAPCON in Washington, D.C. The Federal Library Network (FED-LINK) provides service to federal libraries everywhere although some federal libraries may be acquiring service through their local regional networks. These differing structures are reflected in the types of contracts which the networks offer their own participants.

One essential difference between the networks is that some are composed of users who are members of a formal organization in the sense that they pay membership fees, have voting rights, etc. For this paper, that type of user will be considered a "member." In the other type of network, of which SUNY is an example, the regional network is governed by the policies of the state agency (e.g., the policies of the Board of Trustees of SUNY) and by the state laws and regulations governing the operation of the state agency. In this case, user libraries will be called "network participants."

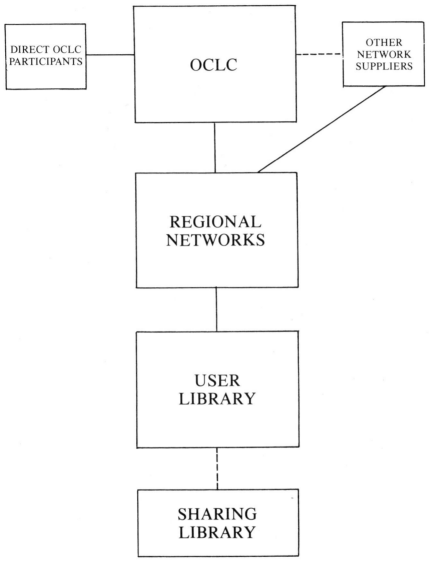

FIGURE 1. CONTRACTUAL LINKS

Regional Network Services

Before considering the contracts, it is necessary to understand the range of services which a regional network supplies to its users.

1. *Implementation and start-up* — telecommunication links planned. For most networks OCLC does this, but for others (e.g., SUNY) the network makes the arrangements through the state agency responsible for the statewide telecommunications network. This entails ordering the installation of modems and synchronizing modem installation with terminal delivery and installation. Also involved here is supervision of line planning and line utilization. The network then trains library personnel in the completion of a profile (for catalog card production), edits the profile, and codes the Pack Definition Table (an intermediate step prior to entry into the OCLC computer) before forwarding the profile to OCLC.
2. *Training and education* — for library administrators and appropriate professional and support staff. Work-flow, integration of the terminal into library operations, MARC formats, tagging practice, ISBD, and current cataloging rules are taught, as well as terminal use, installation, staffing requirements, performance expectations, recordkeeping, etc. There is also instruction in new system procedures and new sub-systems.
3. *Documentation* — to be made available from OCLC or other networks or generated where necessary.
4. *Liaison services* — daily telephone question-answering services on system and cataloging procedures, letter query services, continuing education, and advisory groups (both OCLC and network).
5. *Fiscal relationship* — establish and maintain billing, accounting and auditing procedures with user libraries.
6. *Legal relationship* — establish and maintain contracts with OCLC and user libraries.

Figure 2 illustrates the service relationship links between the telephone company and OCLC, network, user, and sharing library. Fees for services (solid line) are paid by sharing libraries to "users." The combined fees are paid to the "network." After deducting charges for network services, fees are paid to OCLC (and perhaps to the telephone company, depending on regional contractual arrangement). OCLC in turn pays its bills for telephone service, terminal purchase, terminal maintenance, etc.

On-line services are indicated in the figure by a broken line. The user library is directly connected to OCLC computers, and for daily service relationships concerning mechanical terminal or communication problems, works directly with the engineering staff at OCLC. (The network office may have a terminal — most do — for training and liaison purposes, but for the sake of simplicity this relationship is omitted from the figure.)

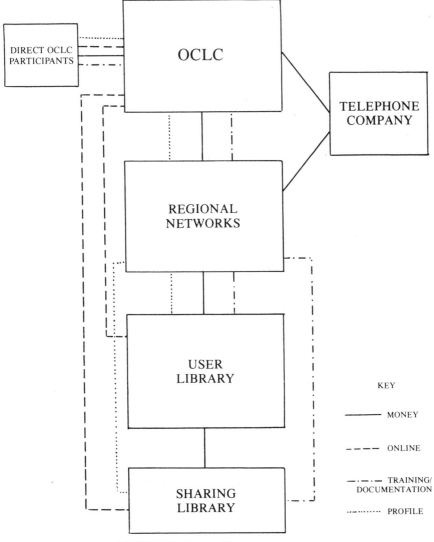

FIGURE 2. SERVICE RELATIONSHIPS

Training, education and documentation services are indicated with the dash-dot line. Some documentation comes from OCLC, and some training is given to network staff. However, the major relationships exist between the network and the user. SUNY estimates that about 70 percent of its effort goes into this activity. Both users and sharers are trained equally and receive the same documentation.

The profile activity (dotted line) begins as negotiation between the regional networks and both users and sharers. Results of this work are forwarded to OCLC. It should be noted that libraries are not static organizations, and profile changes are a continuing activity after the library is established as a member of the network.

The network office performs the major planning, scheduling and coordinating role for both the user libraries and the network as a whole. The contract between network and library must specify the relationships and responsibilities in the provision of these services to the libraries in the network.

Fiscal Support of Regional Networks

Networks are supported by a variety of fiscal sources including grants and local, state and federal funds. In some cases, income is also derived from membership fees and annual dues. Most income is derived from service charges to the libraries. These charges can be indirect, such as a surcharge placed on OCLC services (on the FTU charge), or assessed directly as a charge for network services, such as the "administrative overhead" charged by SUNY. The types and amounts of charges will be specified in the contract between the network and the user.

Libraries Served by Regional Networks

As the regional networks vary in their governance structures, so do the libraries contracting for service. These differences must be accounted for in the contracts. Some libraries are associated with public higher education and are either state- or city-governed. Private higher education and other private institutions such as museums, learned societies, etc., have their own boards of trustees. Community colleges and public library systems will operate within state, county or city regulations. State agency libraries which require service must conform their contracts to state requirements. As expected, the requirements of one federal agency are not necessarily the same as those of another. Some libraries of profit-making institutions are sometimes able to obtain services from regional networks.

Translation of Network Services and Structures into a Contract

At this point, it is necessary to bring together the foregoing discussion (OCLC services, network services, network financing, and library administrative structures) to examine the contracts which have been devised to provide network services.

A review of several network contracts reveals great similarity among their expressions of essential purpose, with variations depending on individual regional network needs. Some of these variations are:
1. Contracts generally make OCLC services available during the life of the network contract with OCLC, with provision for extension.

2. Those networks which require library membership for participation may include membership clauses within the contract. PRLC's contract contains an example of such a clause: "Library shall participate in the OCLC, through the auspices of PRLC, subject to the terms and conditions herein provided. Participation shall be subject to and shall include the following: . . . becoming a voting member of PRLC and paying annual dues and the OCLC participation fee."

3. Networks have a standard contract which many libraries will be able to sign with no variation and, if necessary, the standard contract can be varied to meet the individual library's needs.

4. The particular method of network financing is embedded in the contract. These financing methods are: administering a separately designated charge, adding a surcharge on service charges, or a combination of both.

In the sense that there is a degree of similarity in the contracts and that an examination of one is useful, a detailed review of the basic SUNY contract follows.

WITNESSETH:

WHEREAS, State University of New York and the Ohio College Library Center (OCLC) have concluded a contract under which participating libraries may obtain from the Ohio College Library Center on-line computer library services,

and,

WHEREAS, all libraries which participate in this contract seek to work together in the development of a common on-line bibliographic network; and

WHEREAS, the libraries of State University and other not-for-profit institutions in the State of New York are to be participating members in the network; and

WHEREAS, the Ohio College Library Center will make available to State University and participating members its on-line shared cataloging service and supporting off-line services; and

WHEREAS, State University of New York will make available its facilities such that libraries may use that service, as it is offered by OCLC; and

WHEREAS, in order to do this State University of New York will contract with participating libraries in order to make available such service to those libraries, during the life of its contract with OCLC.

Note the limitation to the libraries of not-for-profit institutions, a present requirement of the policies of the Board of Trustees.

NOW, THEREFORE, the parties hereto agree as follows:

1. State University shall make available an on-line shared monograph cataloging library service to USER, including making available machine readable cataloging records on-line and making available the production and furnishing of off-line catalog card production services.

2. The charge for service to USER will be based on calls made on the Ohio College Library Center system for card production by USER where the data requested is found within the data bank. No charge will be made in those cases in which data shall have been introduced by the requesting library nor for use beyond first-time use of data from another institution. Such a call, sometimes referred to as a "hit," will be charged at the amount charged to State University by OCLC.

In Clause 2, the last sentence establishes the principle of charging to the user the charges made by OCLC. In this case, network income is derived from a separately identified charge (see Clause 5).

3. State University will make available such new services as, from time to time, it is able to secure from OCLC, for such additional charges, and on such a basis as may be required by the agreement between State University and OCLC, and subject to an additional or amended contract between State University and USER.

This clause makes it very easy for both network and library to use the expanding services of OCLC by simple amendment of the appendix containing the fee structure.

4. State University will make available to USER the OCLC Model 100 display terminal for purchase by USER, at the price paid by State University for such terminal; the USER will thereafter maintain the same at USER's own cost and expense.

Here again, the exact cost is passed on to the participant. This clause also identifies OCLC as the sole supplier of a terminal unique to the system. This is a very valuable clause for libraries of governmental agencies that are restricted to competitive bidding situations for supplies and equipment. This clause also identifies the user's responsibility for terminal maintenance.

5. State University will make available advisory services, instruction and training, prepare catalog profile questionnaire and will provide follow-up support services as required. An additional charge for the above services shall be payable by USER monthly to State University in accordance with the schedule as specified in Appendix I, which is attached hereto and made a part hereof.

This clause identifies the network services provided to the participants by State University. All network income for service is authorized in this clause, in the appendix and in the profile charge authorized in Clause 7.

6. USER shall be responsible to State University for monthly payment for communication circuits through which the USER will participate in the on-line shared cataloging system. Such costs shall be prorated by dividing the total number of terminals using the State University data links with OCLC by the total cost of these links as charged by Common Carrier and allocating the cost equally per terminal. The communication costs and additional charges for leased telephone equipment, including data sets, will be payable monthly to State University.

Note the charging mechanism used to compute telephone communication charges. It was very strongly felt that a library joining the network should not be penalized with larger telecommunication charges by reason of geographical remoteness, or have an advantage from location in an urban area. This charging method was accepted by the libraries and has worked satisfactorily. Note also that, with the exception of FEDLINK, all other networks pay OCLC for phone services.

7. USER shall be responsible for payment to State University of certain one time start-up costs, including the installation of telephone data service and essential programming by State University and OCLC staff for catalog card formats. Charges from other agencies shall be passed on to USER at cost as they are billed to State University.

8. USER agrees that, regardless of when actual services shall commence, USER shall reimburse State University for all costs actually incurred for USER's benefit hereunder, from the date first above written throughout the term of this agreement. It is further agreed that, in the event USER terminates this agreement at any time, USER shall remain responsible for payment for all services rendered through the date of termination, and for all maintenance required.

9. USER may request magnetic tapes containing catalog records produced by USER in MARC format at cost as billed to State University.

10. This agreement shall remain in effect only during the life of the State University of New York contract with the Ohio College Library Center. Either party may terminate this agreement on 120 days notice.

11. Any notice to either party hereunder must be in writing, signed by the party giving it, and shall be served either personally or by registered mail addressed as follows:

TO STATE UNIVERSITY:

    Vice Chancellor for Finance and Business
    State University of New York
    99 Washington Avenue
    Albany, New York 12210

TO USER:

or to such addressee as may be hereafter designated by notice. All notices become effective only when received by the addressee.

12. Accounts and bills will be paid under procedures established by SUNY Central Administration in accord with usual practice.

13. USER hereby agrees to abide by such network data standards as are agreed to or as may be agreed to from time to time, and are incorporated in the SUNY-OCLC contract.

The OCLC document "Standards for Input Cataloging" is an appendix to the SUNY/OCLC contract; that is, the regional network agreed to abide by those standards. This clause binds the participant in that agreement.

14. USER agrees to hold harmless and indemnify State University and the State of New York, from and against any claim which may arise out of the use of the equipment or services provided hereunder, unless such claim shall arise out of the willful negligence of the State University, its officers or employees.

15. Current charges for OCLC and SUNY services are specified in Appendix I. All future charges are subject to change by State University upon 60 days written notice to USER. USER shall either accept new charges or decline further service, by written response to State University within the 60 day notice period.

16. Exhibit A, attached hereto, is made a part hereof, and where applicable shall be binding upon USER.

Exhibit A, not reproduced here, is a SUNY "boiler plate" statement concerning such requirements as Workmen's Compensation Act, nonassignment of contract, affirmative action, tax status of the state of New York, and noncollusive bidding.

Affixed to the contracts are the signatures of the library (or its administrative officer), the university, the Attorney-General's office and the state comptroller, thus making the contract formal and binding between the state of New York and the library.

Although contracts between user libraries and sharing libraries are purely private arrangements beyond the purview of the network, they are interesting and appropriate for consideration here.

The development of network services for small groups of sharing libraries is an intriguing phenomenon, in part because of the variety of approaches which have been tried and found workable. In some cases, one library will acquire a terminal and provide a remote catalog service for one or more libraries, taking up spare capacity on its own terminal. In other cases, an institution will establish itself as a service center to provide services to smaller libraries in its region. Capital District 3R's in Rensselaer, New York, for instance, provides service to Schenectady Community College, Fulton-Montgomery Community College, Union College, SUNY Cobleskill Agricultural and Technical College, and Albany Law School. The libraries transmit worksheets and copies of the title pages, etc., to CDLC where they are entered in the system there. Catalog cards go directly to the libraries. The service's effectiveness is demonstrated by the fact that Albany Law School is reclassifying its library using this technique.

The other method commonly used by sharing libraries is one in which terminals are made available to other libraries at specified times. This technique was pursued in Alfred, New York, where the College of Ceramics and Alfred Agriculture & Technology used time on the terminal at Alfred University. A similar arrangement is being developed between St. Joseph College and both St. Francis College and Pratt Institute in Brooklyn.

Following are outlines of letters of agreement to demonstrate the typical provisions in sharing contracts. The first is between Medical Library Center (MLC) of New York and its eleven members using the shared catalog service.[1] MLC will: (1) serve as parent institution; (2) assist in profiling; (3) provide staff orientation (with SUNY/OCLC); (4) enter catalog data supplied by the library into the OCLC system, supply cards, and include the library in composite holdings tape; and (5) provide management support. The library will: (1) process x titles in current fiscal year; (2) send personnel to training; (3) follow established procedures; (4) accept, without revision, ISBD-M; (5) accept LC or NLM subject heading format; (6) send representatives to meetings of Shared Catalog Service; (7) accept charges assessed in accord with financial plan; and (8) have the option of terminating the agreement upon 90 days notice from either party.

The second type of letter of agreement, e.g., the St. Joseph/St. Francis/ Pratt Institute contract, specifies that St. Joseph (the terminal-owning library) will make the terminal available to the other libraries "for 12 hours in prime time" in any week; that the libraries will share in OCLC costs as charged by SUNY; that the three libraries will work cooperatively in developing work-flow patterns and in experimenting with various methods of operation in order to achieve maximum efficiency and cost effectiveness. Finally, the agreement recognizes the need for flexibility due to new and changing operational conditions and the need to evaluate procedures during the year.

Sharing arrangements have worked well, and in fact, have often led to acquisition by one of the sharing libraries of its own terminal as it realizes the potential for services beyond cataloging. When that happens, the library negotiates a direct network contract, although much of the work (profiling, training, etc.) will have been done through its sharing status.

Problems Encountered in Contracting with Libraries

Institutions which are government-based may have bidding requirements for the purchase of services or equipment. That OCLC is a sole-source operation, and that its terminal is unique to the system (as noted above) considerably simplify the procedures for the acquisition of services by its libraries. In New York it is necessary to demonstrate to the Bureau of Audit and Control (as SUNY did) that the terminal is unique. There is no such constraint with printer attachments, however, other than the general provision that they need to be approved by OCLC. Here there may be a state or local contract for the acquisition of printer terminals which might restrict the library's choice. No such restraint is placed on private institutions, of course.

Many state, local and federal agencies will require a clause to be added to the contract authorizing and specifying an upper limit on expenditure. The following example is from the city of Rochester's contract:

It is expressly understood by all parties to this agreement that the user shall be liable only to the total extent, not to exceed $30,962, which has been authorized by the City Council of Rochester on May 14, 1974, under Ordinance #74-141, for the purpose that portions of such monies have been approved by such City Council.

Agencies may add clauses specifying policies relating to invoices or FOB destination, etc. Some will require that different segments of the service be charged to different internal contract numbers, e.g., FTU's have one number, telecommunications another. Different fiscal years may present a problem, not so much in the contract as in its administration, particularly where estimates of expenditure are concerned. At present, SUNY, which has an April-March fiscal year, deals with others which have fiscal years beginning in April, July, September and October. It is also necessary to have a valid state contract number on the contracts (which involves the approvals and signatures noted above) before the libraries can pay bills under the contract. Some difficulty has been caused in synchronizing the completion of the contract processing with the commencement of service.

In addition to bidding requirements some networks have additional needs. For example, NELINET acquired some Spiras terminals (used in the OCLC network before the development of the OCLC/Beehive Model 100) and subsequently took over their parts inventory to provide terminal maintenance. Their user contract would reflect this activity. Occasional contracts have been arranged in which equipment is leased for a short period rather than purchased by the library. Usually in those cases, the library also accepts terminal maintenance responsibility and costs. With regard to terminal maintenance, some networks favor the "per call" method of billing, others the monthly charge. It is understood, however, that OCLC will discontinue the "per call" charge option in the near future. It should be noted that the terminals are quite stable, a stability which is reflected by the decrease in terminal maintenance charges from $47.50 per month in 1975-76 to $33.00 per month in 1977-78.

Obviously, sometimes things happen which cause upset, misunderstanding and delay. In general, such instances are indicative of unfamiliarity with contracting procedures (data processing contracts in particular) on the part of librarians. In the hope of avoiding these problem areas, a few are listed here:

1. Do not annotate any copy of the contract with notes like "See Charlie about this" or "Prices reduced next year" if you plan to sign and notarize that copy of the contract. Such annotations on a signed contract are amehdments.
2. Do not sign subsidiary agreements (i.e., terminal maintenance) that have been appended and marked "for information and exhibition only."
3. Have the signatures notarized.
4. Make sure that the signator has the authority to sign on behalf of the institution.
5. Remember that the network is relatively powerless to change appendixes and exhibits to contracts between OCLC and a third party, at least in time to process the contract. In other words, try not to amend them before signing the contract. The same is true of tariffs which are set by the Federal Communications Commission for telecommunications.

Attention to these details will hasten the processing of the library's contract, reduce the load on network staff, and reduce the costs of running the network — all to the library's benefit.

This paper has reviewed the contractual relationships which exist between OCLC regional networks and its user libraries, and looked briefly at the subsidiary contracts made between users and sharing libraries. Negotiation is not a major force in the development of such contracts;

rather, the emphasis in the contracting process has been on the differing environments of both networks and libraries, and on the need to accommodate these varying needs in the contract. Personal experience indicates that these discussions are usually good-natured and that, for the most part, users and networks are satisfied with the responsibilities embodied in user contracts for the OCLC system.

Gratitude is expressed here to those libraries and networks which granted permission for direct quotation or paraphrase from their contracts in this paper, and to those regional networks affiliated with OCLC which made copies of their standard contracts available.

REFERENCE

1. Raper, James E., Jr., "Centralized Automated Cataloging of Health Science Materials in the MLC/SUNY/OCLC Shared Cataloging Service," *Bulletin of the Medical Library Association* 65:231-42, April 1977.

BRUCE D. BAJEMA
County Librarian
Marin County Free Library
San Rafael, California

Negotiating for Innovative Service

EVEN IN THE BEST of circumstances, where the product is easily definable and there is a plentitude of suppliers, contracts can be difficult. The minute one moves into the computer world with its infinite variety of hardware, software and combinations thereof, the difficulties grow geometrically. Add the factor of a new product to the combination and the odds might appear insurmountable. However, by the end of this paper, I trust that the reader will have gained an idea at least of the process used in this one instance to negotiate a contract for an innovative service.

The key to success in this kind of venture is finding a vendor who is trustworthy and willing to adapt, change and be creative in the problem-solving process. The product has to be viewed as a joint effort with mutual benefits. Try to avoid the "us-versus-them" syndrome.

The Setting

Marin is a well-to-do county located just north of San Francisco. The people there have a high per capita income, are well educated and generally support educational institutions very well. Marin County has a population of 216,000 spread over an area of 600 square miles in a sub-urban-rural mix. There are 5 city libraries serving about 86,000 people. The remaining 130,000 people, spread over 560 square miles, fall within the county library's service area, which encompasses 6 incorporated cities or towns and 12 villages scattered in the unincorporated rural area. To serve this area there are a central library, three large branches, two small branches, six stations and a bookmobile. In FY 1977, the library had an operating budget of $1,462,000, with a staff of fifty-five full-time employees plus five CETA employees.

The History

In 1972 the County Administrator's Office (CAO), the personnel department and the county librarian agreed to a personnel audit of all positions. The audit suggested that a policy of promoting public access to any and all materials desired was creating a demand for materials which was growing at a steady arithmetic rate, while the staff time needed to handle the additional workload was increasing at a much faster rate. The geometric increase in workload was caused by: (1) an increase in requests, (2) growing files, and (3) a growing complexity of requests. The personnel findings led to a recommendation to the CAO that certain functions be automated. This in turn led to a self-administered, detailed task-time study of one month's duration. The study provided the hard data necessary to do cost comparison analysis preliminary to installation of any new system. It also reinforced the CAO's authorization to "go ahead and automate as long as it doesn't take any programming manpower from the County Data Processing Department."

The Problem

Our short-term problem was to come up with an automated system which would either stop or reverse the geometric increase in staff time needed to maintain and search the bibliographic files. The long-term goal was to design the bibliographic phase so that it would be an integral part of an overall system, including selection, acquisition, cataloging, circulation and inventory control.

The apparent solution to the short-term problem was a union catalog in book form, with production and maintenance performed by a computer utilizing a machine-readable data base. This, in turn, presented a number of questions: (1) Should we use a vendor or do the work in-house? (2) If the work were done in-house, where would programs be obtained? (3) Should the backfile be converted or ignored? (4) If the backfile were converted, how would it be done? and (5) Would new records be added to the file by keying in-house, or by extracting LC MARC records, or by having a vendor key the records? All these concerns may seem to be quite removed from contract negotiation; however, each of them helped to shape the final contract.

The Search

With an automated book catalog as the goal, the search began. First, other California libraries which were actively automating some process were surveyed. This survey, which consisted of on-site visits whenever possible and telephone calls when they were not, lasted about eight months. During this time it became apparent that a catalog in microform was cheaper and better from the standpoint of flexibility, so the hard-copy book catalog idea was dropped. The decisions which evolved from the survey were:

1. A catalog in microform would be produced.
2. A vendor would be employed to perform ongoing maintenance, update the files, produce the catalog, and maintain the data base.
3. The initial backfile conversion would be accomplished by matching Marin County's "location file" (a main entry file in alphabetical order with holdings and location indicated) with an existing machine-readable data base.
4. Once the conversion was begun, all new titles would go into the microform catalog.
5. The card catalogs would be closed.
6. The remaining backfile would be converted as replacements were ordered and received, and as time and money became available.
7. The data base would be LC MARC compatible and, if returned to us for other use, would be in the MARC communications format.

With those decisions made, it was necessary to look for a vendor who could attempt two innovative processes within the single overall system. At that time, neither backfile conversion using an existing data base nor the microform catalog for a complete public library collection had yet been tried. The initial contact was a brief letter to three or four known vendors of book catalogs to express our desire to convert the backfile and produce a microform catalog. This was followed by personal contacts with three of the vendors at the California Library Association (CLA) annual conference. After the conference, a more detailed letter that spelled out the microform possibilities, the conversion process desired and the LC MARC compatibility requirement was sent to five vendors (all of whom had produced book catalogs from bibliographic data bases) to request estimated unit prices for the conversion process. The procedures and responses varied.

The first vendor (Vendor A) received a County Librarian (CL)-originated letter, followed by a telephone call. There was a conversation (county-originated) at the CLA conference, followed by another telephone call from CL and, finally, another letter. There was no response from the vendor to any of these initiatives.

The second vendor (Vendor B) received a letter from CL, and responded with three or four conversations and/or telephone calls. The result was a proposal from the vendor to keypunch a search key which would be matched against the LC MARC file. The price quoted was for the total job without a breakdown per item. We were, however, looking for a per unit cost in order to maintain maximum control.

The third vendor (Vendor C) received a letter from CL and responded with a telephone call. The county then initiated a personal contact at the CLA conference and followed it with a letter. The vendor responded to this effort with another telephone call. The result was a proposal to convert the total file by keypunching a search for matching and complete keypunching of all the nonmatches. The vendor was unwilling to allow us to do the matching in-house, and wanted to do the complete file as a package. They did not understand the fiscal constraints of the project, nor the need for in-house control of some aspects of the conversion.

The fourth vendor (Vendor D) participated in a conversation during the CLA conference, and strongly advised against a film catalog: "A book catalog is the only solution; the public will not use a microform catalog." (Today this vendor is advertising microfilm catalogs.)

The fifth vendor (Vendor E) received a more detailed letter spelling out the project and requesting quotes, and responded by telephone. Three and one-half months passed without any contact, and then the vendor's new department head made another telephone call. The vendor visited the library and gathered a sample of titles. This was followed by another telephone call from the vendor reporting on ultrafiche versus fiche or roll film costs — with a recommendation not to buy ultrafiche. As a result, a good proposal was developed by the vendor dealing with most of the local concerns based on staged conversion and production. Their price was competitive with the sixth vendor. However, inasmuch as they had "lost" the file on this project for three and one-half months, there was concern about their consistency and dependability.

A visit from the sixth vendor (Vendor F) resulted in a long discussion about backfile conversion strategies. This contact was followed by a letter to the vendor, two or three telephone calls from CL, and another letter outlining additional details vis-à-vis the library's requirements. The vendor then made another visit. The resulting proposal provided unit prices for conversion with a range of prices (dependent on how much was done by the library and how much by the vendor). Production prices were based on the number of frames printed, with control of length and format of entries to be the complete responsibility of the library. Charges were specified for current additions by either vendor or library, as were prices for corrections/deletions.

Concurrent with the vendor search, the county purchasing agent was consulted as to the advisability of going to bid with a very specific document as opposed to a general contract to be signed after the vendor was selected and prices agreed upon. He raised the following questions:

1. Could we define the product exactly enough to include specifics in a bid document?
2. Was this an established product with a number of suppliers?
3. Was there a vendor who would sign a contract with no minimum guarantee and with the county controlling production?
4. Was the library staff competent to determine whether a satisfactory product was delivered at the specified unit pricing?

After considerable discussion it was agreed to use a short general contract and to attach a letter of understanding which would include unit prices. This was arrived at through the following rationale:

1. With the county controlling input and production cycles, there would be comparatively little financial exposure.
2. By not spelling out the product exactly, we could add, delete, modify or even change formats in order to get the best working product within the dollar constraints at any time.
3. This would also be an incentive for the vendor to improve the processes and/or the product as we could accept the changes and improvements without amending the contract document each time.
4. This flexibility would be of major benefit to the county in that change could be made as technology advanced.
5. This form of contract would require a good deal of communication on a regular basis which would in turn lead to more satisfaction on both sides and a better product.

Negotiation

Most of the negotiations took place during the end of the vendor search period. In meetings and telephone conversations, as the concepts and implementation strategies were discussed and worked out, unit prices would be one of the points of discussion. These were usually approached both from what the county considered a reasonable price and what the vendor could live with while still making a profit. As prices surfaced, library staff cross-checked with county data processing and/or a vendor of a similar service. For example, it was very easy to run down a variety of per fiche reproduction costs depending on frequency and volume. When the price seemed satisfactory, county staff indicated this to the vendor(s); if the price seemed out of line, discussions resumed until agreement was reached. During this time, the following costs were found to be those needed in order for the county to maintain fiscal control of the project:

1. production costs of COM master to be quoted as a per frame price (including all computer time, tapes, etc.);
2. unit cost of adding a record;
3. unit cost of correcting or deleting a record;
4. unit cost of duplicating the microform catalog;

5. unit cost of extracting backfile records in the initial conversion;
6. unit cost of re-exploding the complete file;
7. start-up costs;
8. the estimated cost of a built-in requirement allowing the library to get a copy of the data at any time; and
9. ending costs.

Vendor Decision and Contract

We finally narrowed our search to vendors C, E and F. The pricing structure of Vendor C was unsatisfactory, as the total cost included only the first edition of the catalog and a probable ongoing cost. Moreover, this vendor had a strong commitment to roll film, and we hadn't decided yet between roll film and fiche. Vendors E and F had very similar costs for conversion and ongoing production. Vendor E had a slight edge in potential backfile titles available (about 5 percent); however, the lackadaisical attitude in presenting a proposal (plus the fact that the employee who had rescued the file was leaving) left us with some trepidation about the vendor's ability to perform. Vendor F remained, and as we came to an understanding of procedures, process and price, we asked this vendor for a formal proposal spelling out the costs and other details.

County library staff then requested county counsel to draft a very simple contract (see Appendix) spelling out our requirements and referring to the vendor's proposal which was then attached to the contract. The proposal and the contract were so easy at this point that they were almost anticlimactic. This simple contract and proposal have served us well, however; the first contract written for one year with monthly extensions lasted twenty-four months, at which time a similar 3-year contract was signed.

Provisions Not Covered by the Contract

This kind of contract may leave a number of items not covered, and both parties must be aware of this and willing to work on developing the best end product. The following items were not mentioned in our contract: (1) film format, (2) text format, (3) data elements included, (4) number of catalogs, (5) production frequency, (6) supplemental catalogs, (7) penalties or time constraints, (8) reduction ratio, (9) how or from where data are to be delivered, and (10) cross-reference file.

Conclusion

In order for this kind of process to work successfully, a number of factors must be observed:

1. One must be honest and open with vendors, particularly in letting them know that other vendors are being considered as well.
2. Vendors should be informed when a decision is made and why.

3. The library staff must understand pricing structures and have a good grasp of the potential of the technology to be used.
4. Deadlines must be established and kept, even though this is not a formal bid process.
5. There must be trust and an understanding that the relationship will be one of mutual benefit.
6. Both parties must realize that there is a number of items to be worked out or experimented with during the term of the contract.
7. Both sides must realize that compromises will have to be made, but that they should be made with the best, most usable end product within the price constraints as the goal.
8. The vendor cannot be expected to lose money and continue to exist.

APPENDIX

AGREEMENT

THIS AGREEMENT, made and entered into this 11th day of June 1974, by and between the COUNTY OF MARIN, a Political Subdivision of the State of California, hereinafter referred to as "COUNTY" and "_____," hereinafter referred to as "CONTRACTOR":

WITNESSETH:

In consideration of the mutual covenants and conditions contained herein, the parties agree:

1. "CONTRACTOR" will produce microfilm catalogues for "COUNTY's" library in accordance with "CONTRACTOR's" proposal, dated May 1, 1974, a copy of which is attached and made a part hereof.

2. "CONTRACTOR" shall be paid monthly for work accomplished on the basis of billings approved by County's Librarian. All work shall be compensated at the rates set forth in the aforementioned proposal.

3. The quantity of work shall be determined by the amount of material transmitted to "CONTRACTOR" by "COUNTY" for transfer to microfilm. It is specifically understood and agreed that "COUNTY" is not obligated to transmit any minimum amount of material. "COUNTY's" decision as to the amount of work to be done, in any month or pursuant to the entire contract shall be final.

4. This Agreement shall remain in effect for a period of one year from June 11, 1974 to June 11, 1975. Thereafter the Agreement shall be deemed automatically extended for additional periods of thirty (30) days unless either party gives the other written notice to the contrary.

5. It is specifically understood and agreed that, while rendering services hereunder, "CONTRACTOR" is an independent contractor, not any agent of "COUNTY" for any purpose whatsoever.

IN WITNESS WHEREOF, the parties have entered into this Agreement the day and year first above written.

COUNTY OF MARIN

By_____
                "COUNTY"

By_____
              "CONTRACTOR"

CHARLES DYER

Assistant Professor of Law
Saint Louis University
St. Louis, Missouri

Data Processing Contracts: A Tutorial

NO ONE CAN ADEQUATELY condense the immense field of contract law into a short speech or paper. Expertise in contract law should be left to lawyers. A librarian who attempted to learn contract law would be wasting his time because it is so easy to hire professional help on those rare occasions when it's needed. Contract *negotiations,* however, are a different matter. No lawyer is trained in law school to understand the ramifications of contract negotiation for data processing services, especially in a library. The technical aspects of the anticipated contract, as opposed to the legal aspects, are usually beyond the comprehension of attorneys. Attorneys generally rely on the businessmen involved, i.e., the vendor and the librarian, to anticipate the technical problems that may arise in contract negotiations. In order to understand fully all the implications of technology in the contractual setting, however, the librarian must know some basics of contract law and possible contract clauses.

The speech at the 1977 clinic on which this paper is based was intended to be an introduction to contract law for the purpose of conducting a practicum in contract negotiations. The aim of the practicum was to present a situation as close to an actual contractual environment as possible. A turnkey circulation system was used as the example, since that is perhaps the form of data processing most commonly entered into first. The proposal given in Appendix A is somewhat limited in technical statements to ensure that the practicum participants could discuss them all in the time allowed. The standard form contract given in Appendix B is a composite of several contracts presently being used by vendors of library systems. The content is typical of library turnkey system contracts in both language and length. It is also typical in that there are provisions that may not be in the best interests of the library. A wise librarian would want to suggest changes, possibly in accordance with some of the suggestions made in this paper. This paper will be easier to follow if the reader refers to the appendixes for examples of problems delineated here.

EXISTENCE OF OBLIGATION

In reviewing contract law, it is best to begin with certain basics. The discussion will begin at the negotiating stage rather than at some later time after mistakes have been discovered. Ordinarily, one need not worry about unwittingly creating an obligation (a "contract") with a vendor. Nevertheless, it *can* happen; for instance, a letter to the vendor, stating: "I like your proposal. We accept it just as it is," might be construed by a court as acceptance of a contractual offer, even though there was never any formal discussion with the vendor about delivery, installation date, warranties, and so on.[1] A letter, stating: "I like your proposal except that there are a few points I want clarified and I want a more extended payment period," could be construed as a counter-offer. If the vendor replies, "All right, I agree to everything you say; let's get that machine in there," then he is accepting your counter-offer. Although this is not a formal contract, it is nevertheless a contract.[2]

The basic rule is not to deal too fast. Do not say that you will take it as you see it. Sit down and talk with the vendor; make no final commitments without arrangements for warranties, delivery dates, and all the things that are part of a good contract. The last thing to do is to have a vendor rely (to his detriment) on promises or expectations of business. The court may create a contractual obligation simply through failure to deny.

ENFORCEMENT OF OBLIGATION

The enforcement of obligation may seem remote during contract negotiation, but the real purpose of a contract is to establish the rules for the enforcement of obligation.

The Parol Evidence Rule

Perhaps the most heartbreaking rule for a novice data processing purchaser is the parol evidence rule. "Parol" means oral; oral evidence about a written contract does not stand up in court. The law presumes that a written agreement contains all the terms of that agreement. Thus, the parol evidence rule also includes written statements made prior to the contract. Many standard form contracts contain a clause that all statements, oral and written, made outside the contract are not pertinent.[3]

Occasionally, parol evidence can be valid if it is made after the contract has been signed.[4] For instance, the vendor may say: "Look, I have a cancellation of another contract. I can deliver two months earlier. Why don't you gear up ahead of time?" The librarian assents and hires expensive staff to begin on the new starting date. Under these circumstances, if the vendor fails to deliver by the new date, the librarian can probably recover. There is still the problem of proof. If a change is made subsequent to the signing of the contract, any conversation should be followed by a letter spelling out exactly the new terms agreed upon.

The basic problem with the parol evidence rule is that it eliminates the proposal as part of the evidence of the obligation.[5] In a typical situation there are differences between a proposal and a contract. (Note the differences between the proposal and contract included in the appendixes, taking into account the terms added under the vendor's instructions, Appendix C, before the negotiations began.)

In the case of *Lovable Co.* v. *Honeywell, Inc.,*[6] Lovable, a brassiere manufacturer, had an attractive proposal from Honeywell for a data processing system. The U.S. Court of Appeals for the Fifth Circuit ruled that Lovable failed to include a letter from Honeywell in the contract. In their letter, Honeywell guaranteed that the system would work. Since that was not in the contract, all that Honeywell really guaranteed when they sold the system to Lovable was that the machines would arrive. Although this case occurred in 1970 (when courts still thought of computers as fancy typewriters), such a ruling could be made today. The clause in the Lovable contract disallowing parol evidence is still common in contracts.

Breach of Contract

Perhaps the best way to avoid problems of enforcement of obligation is to find a good vendor in the first place. A one-page contract is sufficient with a vendor whose performance is known. Unfortunately, such certainty is rare. The fact that a vendor has been selling good library supplies for some time does not mean that the data processing department, made up of a completely different staff handling a completely different product, will perform as capably. Similarly, if the library systems department of a big computer vendor makes no money, it will be scuttled for more profitable endeavors, leaving the library with a computer without upkeep or support.

Nevertheless, any reputable dealer who feels able to perform will have no qualms about signing a contract. The vendor can easily say what he intends to do if he really intends to do it. Vendors who squirm or try to avoid contract negotiation are cause for concern. Some vendor salesmen claim they are not allowed to discuss contract terms; ask to speak to someone who can.

All states except Louisiana have adopted the Uniform Commercial Code, a set of rules that simplifies and facilitates business transactions. Something that under the old rule used to constitute a breach of contract by its mere occurrence may no longer constitute a breach. Under the old laws, for example, late delivery constituted breach, and consequently permitted the receiver to avoid discharging his own obligations (such as paying for the shipment). Under the UCC, the court may not allow that.[7] If the delivery were, for instance, a week late and nothing else were different, the court might note the fact that the vendor expended months of effort to get it there and decide that the contract is still in force. Under the UCC, the contract does not have to be performed to the letter. This is good for the business community as it discourages predatory businessmen from signing contracts with the intent of waiting for the other party to make a minor slip. Under the UCC, if the injured party can mitigate his damages, he is expected to do so[8] and to sue (or settle) for an amount related to the extent of the damages.

There can be reasons why deviation from the terms of a contract (e.g., late delivery) is not acceptable; if the reasons are legitimate, the court will listen to them. Arguments made at that time will affect the ultimate settlement. The better the evidence presented in court (proof of the harm caused by late delivery), the better the settlement will be. Unfortunately, libraries, like other state institutions, have a very hard time claiming damages which cannot be put in terms of lost profits or of lost money. Furthermore, the UCC is generally considered to be concerned with products, not services. Insofar as data processing contracts are contracts for services, the UCC is not all that helpful. The emphasis of the UCC on fungibility and mitigation of damages may not help when dealing with the only vendor in town.

Resolving the Contract Dispute

Although this section is not exactly pertinent to contract negotiations, it may help to clarify options available after the fact and to aid in understanding certain contract clauses.

In order to act on another's breach, the legal framework must be observed. In the event of a suspected breach, the offended party must notify the other party.[9] After that there is a number of options, such as stopping the contract. One ought to plan to mitigate damages by seeking another vendor or perhaps by buying part of the materials needed from someone else. If a total system is being purchased, this can be quite a problem. If there had been bargaining for a prolonged arrangement for innovative work (e.g., developing a new system), the buyer might want to go to some other vendor for peripherals.

One can sue for specific performance, which means performance exactly as specified in the contract. Although the layman may think that specific performance is the common remedy, it is actually quite rare for the contracts being considered here. Specific performance is well known because most people become involved in contracts that demand specific performance; for instance, a breach of a contract for land is almost always remedied by specific performance. The traditional feeling of the courts has been that a specific piece of land is unique and that no amount of money will give the same satisfaction as owning that land. Therefore, the courts give the equitable remedy: specific performance.[10] However, for the ordinary dealings between businessmen, when the same product is available from someone else, the courts will not demand specific performance. Even the nonexistence of competitors may not be enough for a court to consider specific performance. A library denied access to OCLC could obviously still build its own cataloging data base using MARC tapes. The court would not begin to think of specific performance in such an instance unless and until it might classify OCLC as a public utility.

The most realistic way to resolve a contract dispute is simply to talk it over with the vendor — to bargain. For instance, if a vendor will be delayed in providing the hardware for a turnkey circulation system, perhaps early delivery of the bar-coded labels for the books can be procured. The library can then gear up that part of the operation and avoid a loss of valuable personnel time.

Contract disputes can be settled by not acting at all, but at some risk. Even if the other party's actions are considered to be a breach, failure to protest can be considered a waiver of rights to press a claim. For example, if the vendor delivers goods which are not quite up to the standards of the contract, the librarian might be tempted to accept them anyway, assuming the vendor will ultimately rectify this breach. Not only is this an unrealistic belief, but mere acceptance of the goods waives the right to have the problem corrected.[11] Acceptance is not the only means of waiving one's rights. A person who simply sits and waits, saying, "Why do they keep delaying? Why do they keep delaying?" and neither sends letters nor makes threatening phone calls, may be waiving his rights. If a person feels his vendor is about to breach, he should tell him so in a formal letter.

Another generally unsatisfactory way to settle a contract dispute is called "estoppel." Consider the following scenario. The vendor calls the library to ask if the librarian anticipates a future need for a particular piece of equipment. Without adequate reflection, the librarian answers that no such need is foreseen. When the need does arise, the vendor says: "Acting on your answer, we disposed of our stock of that item. We now have no obligation to furnish this equipment to you." The essential point here is that the vendor relied to his detriment on the librarian's response. The rule is simply to be cautious in making statements; always consider the consequences of the vendor's acting on a statement.

Discharge of Obligation

The discharge of obligation is obviously best handled by performance, but there are other ways. For instance, the statute of limitations on a contract dispute is, for most contracts, four years from the time of the breach. If a vendor breaches repeatedly, damages are limited only to those breaches which occurred within four years of filing the action. Given the delays that can naturally occur in trying to coax the vendor into performance, four years is not such a long time.

Discharge of obligation may also be due to a change in circumstances. For instance, a library faced with an unexpected increase in circulation may find the bargained-for system inadequate. The library will probably be forced to accept the slow system, because the court will rule that although circumstances have changed, the vendor had no warning. The contract clause stating that the system can handle the circulation rate will have no effect. However, if the librarian had had indications of the increasing rate, the vendor could have been pressed to alter the contract before installation. If necessary, in order to alter this inadvisable contract, the librarian could even have taken his case to court. The vendor need only be stopped from performing to his own detriment.

The final way to discharge obligation on the part of the vendor is to have his contract labeled "impossible" by the court. The vendor must cite why the contract is impossible, e.g., the technology does not exist, the correct raw materials are impossible to obtain, etc. A common reason given is that the key man in the organization has left the company. This happens even to large firms such as IBM because small units within the organization control particular kinds of sales — and the library market is a very small market. In court the vendor would probably lose on such a position. The situation must really be impossible, not just very expensive or unprofitable.[12] Not-impossible situations are labeled "frustration." The court applies these labels in order to create a reasonably equitable policy in dealing with these matters. A frustrated vendor may not perform, but must pay.

WRITING THE CONTRACT

Having concluded a cursory examination of contract law, the parts of a contract may now be discussed (see Appendix B). A standard form contract can be expected for almost anything purchased; it would be inefficient for the vendor to write a new contract for every sale. The vendor may have simply hired an attorney for a week to write a few terms on the back of a purchase order, but thought has gone into it.

Nevertheless, the business is more important to the vendor than obtaining a customer's signature on a piece of paper. The vendor wants the sale. The customer can write his own contract or have the vendor's standard form contract changed. If the vendor needs a lawyer to check the new clauses, he will hire one — provided the sale is big enough. Only a large vendor of small merchandise, such as Sears, would refuse to deviate from a standard form contract. Computer system sales, however, are big enough to force a vendor to bend.

Matters of Fact

Contracts can be divided into matters of fact and matters of law. For most data processing contracts, matters of fact, specifications, schedules and so on are usually included as an exhibit at the end of the contract. Be sure that all the necessary technical data are included.

Technical people are good people; they work hard all their lives, and are much too trusting. Usually one deals with a particular vendor because the library's technical people insist that the vendor has a good product. It may well be that the technical person was convinced by a statement made by the salesman over a cup of coffee. The salesman may have been indulging in puffery, or even making untrue claims, but the technical man believed him. Or, the salesman might convince the technical person that a particular machine is being bought, that it will work as claimed, and that the exhibits are of no concern. The technical person does not care about suits and liabilities or contracts, but only about the product itself. It is the librarian's responsibility to make sure that the technical person's understanding of the product is represented in the exhibits to the contract.

As many of the vendor's technological statements as possible should be included in the contract. Particularly important statements made after the contract was signed could be reflected in the contract by changes or appendixes. If a vendor were to guarantee a certain maximum response time in a letter, and that guarantee were critically important, it would be simple to append the letter to the contract as an exhibit and add a clause in the contract referring to the exhibit. This procedure is more readily acceptable than changing an entire section of the contract just to include the new guarantee. Attachment of exhibits in this way is an easy way to test the sincerity of a salesman's claims.

There should be a lot of concern about how the products are classified. The classification of a piece of machinery as hardware, as opposed to software, can make a sizable difference with respect to litigation. For example, a "smart" terminal may have some programming included in its price, but be described as hardware in the contract. A specific UCC provision may then apply to the terminal as a product rather than as a service provided.[13] Furthermore, the distinction may apply to taxes. In many states software is still not taxable and may remain so for some time. Federal taxes, such as excise taxes, can also be affected by the contractual distinctions. Libraries are not always able to avoid such taxes, especially with rental agreements.

One turnkey circulation system vendor sells the system as one package, making no classification of the parts. Thus, a librarian would avoid the problem Lovable had with Honeywell.[14] On the other hand, the delineation of parts can become important when there is a problem with a specific part. If that specific part needed to be replaced, an obstinate vendor might demand to take the whole package back in order to replace the one part. If the parts are separated on paper, the court will be more inclined to see them as individual items. It is desirable that the contract refer both to the system and to the parts of the system.

Matters of Law

The items needed in a specific contract vary, of course, according to the purpose of the contract. The individual matters of law could be thought to correspond roughly to the titles of the various clauses of the contract, provided the contract has clause titles. Care is needed, however, in forming negotiations based on a standard form contract because, occasionally, a very necessary matter of law may not be mentioned at all in a standard form contract. Clause titles solely cannot be relied on as reminders of all the relevant matters of law. The most common matters of law are given below, but a more exhaustive list can be found in Brandon's *Data Processing Contracts*.[15]

Transfer of title is an unnecessary clause in a rental agreement, but can be vastly important in a sales agreement. Is the title being obtained to both the hardware and software, or to just the hardware? Perhaps the software carries with it a trade secret limitation against resale. On an installment purchase, one may be forced to use the vendor's services in order to replace each tube, let alone modify the hardware.

Delivery charges seem minor but can be substantial; most computer vendors sell FOB the home plant but charge for shipping and insurance without any mention in the contract. Damage in transit can be quite a bother.[16]

The vendor might delegate installation to some third party unless the contract states otherwise. The customer may find installation assigned to a less-than-reputable subcontractor simply because the vendor received a sizable order from a large customer and would rather send staff engineers there.

The purchase agreement itself could be assigned to a bank. In this case, stopping payment because the computer does not work is futile; the system will simply be repossessed by the bank rather than by the vendor. The bank will continue to press for the money because it does not want the machine either. The librarian must sue the vendor, who already has his money, in order to get satisfaction.

Duration of the agreement can be problematical. IBM is noted for writing contracts for long periods of time (e.g., delivery in two years) and including a proviso for termination with three months' notice. A vendor with such a clause can wait until just before or just after installation to give a three-month notice of increases. Care should be taken of clauses hidden elsewhere in the contract, not in the duration clause, which can affect the duration.

A peculiar and difficult problem is the confidentiality of the vendor-supplied software, i.e., the programs that operate the system. The vendor has made a large investment in software development and can protect that investment only if the programs are kept secret from actual and potential competitors. For that reason, the vendor is likely to restrict the buyer's use of the software. A computer operator who worked for Texas Instruments once copied several expensively-developed programs and tried to sell them covertly to Texaco. Unfortunately for him, Texaco was not a reliable fence and turned him over to the authorities. On appeal from his conviction, he tried to argue that all he had stolen were some card decks worth only a few dollars, which is not a felony. The Texas Court of Criminal Appeals ruled that the programs were actually worth $2.5 million and upheld the conviction.[17] One should think twice before purloining a confidential program.

Included with a clause of confidentiality of the software may be restrictions of other sorts. The vendor may own the software outright or give the library a nonexclusive restrictive license to use the software but not to copy it. Thus, although the library owns the software, that ownership is virtually meaningless. The library would not be able to add refinements or special features and might not even be able to sell the software if it sold the system. Some vendors even restrict library personnel from looking at the programs in order to protect the programs' trade secret status.

Actually, there can be a tradeoff between accepting certain responsibilities for the software (and thereby creating a whole new data processing department) or leaving it all in the hands of the vendor, who then has the customer at his mercy with respect to the level of sophistication of data processing support. Creating a new department is expensive. Does the library need that much flexibility and long-range development? On the other hand, asking the vendor to add a new service after installation can be expensive and uncertain. The uncertainty results in part from the possibility that the vendor can move his senior programmers to new projects and leave the library's support in the hands of novices.

An arbitration clause is worth pursuing in contract negotiations, as it could save the library considerable expense. Arbitration also brings dispute resolution out of the atmosphere of litigation and can put reality back into the dealings between the parties. To the courts, a library is just another business. But a library has special concerns — it is service oriented, it has to provide information. Inability to get information can be damaging in ways not assessable in dollars. Arbitration enables the library to present its real needs. (Even arbitration can be avoided if good amendment procedures are included in the contract.)

The "responsibility for enforcement" clause should be clearly understood. This is the traditional clause which saddles the buyer with the vendor's attorney fees if the vendor has to sue for nonpayment. This can create problems if one decides not to pay because the vendor has breached. Some buyers have become more timid about pursuing minor breaches because of this possibility of increased damage claims.

Many contracts also include a clause naming the state under whose law the contract will be construed.[18] For instance, IBM usually names New York. For a party in Illinois, this clause could present difficulties, especially if the local judge suggested that suit in New York might be more sensible. Sending witnesses to New York is expensive. The alternative of going to federal court, when the jurisdictional restrictions are met, is not too pleasant. Federal courts are always overcrowded — as are the state courts in New York. That one clause can add a year's time in court delays.

QUESTIONS OF RISK

Direct v. Indirect Risks

The notion of direct and indirect risks is one taken from Bernacchi and Larsen's *Data Processing Contracts and the Law*.[19] Direct risks are those associated with the failure of technology. Indirect risks are those associated with the consequential events due to that failure. Vendors may accept the responsibility for direct risks, but are loathe to accept indirect risks. The separation of direct and indirect risks can be difficult. For instance, if a library put its catalog into a computer system and the computer lost it, that one failure would have both direct and indirect effects. The failure would cost time and money — a direct effect. If the computer had the only copy of the catalog, then the indirect effect would be even more disastrous.

One data processing purchaser put his bills into an automated billing system. The operator did not realize that as each account was entered, the one previously entered was erased. Consequently, at the end of all that work, only the last record was entered in the system. Fortunately, he still had the paper record, so the loss was held to the direct effects.[20] Had the supposedly duplicate and soon-to-be-dated paper record been thrown away, however, the indirect effect would have been considerable.

Indirect risks can take diverse forms. The standard form contract that Mead Data Central uses to market its LEXIS legal information retrieval system contains a disclaimer for indirect risk. Law librarians were concerned at one time that Mead meant to exclude such risks as electric shocks from the terminals, but Mead's real concern was to exclude the possibility of a suit from a lawyer who lost a case in court due to faulty information obtained from LEXIS.

Nonperformance

The obvious direct risk is nonperformance. The vendor may fail to perform due to management failure or financial problems within the organization. Management failure is most common with contracts for an innovative system. The contract should be written to take into account such possibilities. The pitfalls in a contract with heavy emphasis on delivery schedules should be watched for, however, because one of the most common ways data processing users lose contract battles is from their own nonperformance. If the library fails to be prepared for an on-site preinstallation inspection, the vendor may use that as an excuse for delaying delivery. The games that vendors use are well documented elsewhere and beyond the scope of this paper. The only way to prepare for them is to know the vendor through discussion with other customers and to comprehend fully the responsibilities under the contract.

CONTRACT NEGOTIATION GAME

The best method for attaining expertise in contract negotiations is to get some practice at it, to learn to strike a bargain. Remedies given in a contract should be designed to achieve the objectives of both parties. The practicum held at the clinic worked surprisingly well — so well, in fact, that the materials used for the practicum are appended here. The only rule is that only the person who plays the vendor's role may read Appendix C before the negotiations begin.

REFERENCES

1. *See Servco Equipment Co.* v. *C.M. Lingle Co.,* 487 S.W.2d 869 (Mo. Ct. App. 1972).
2. *See V'Soske* v. *Barwick,* 404 F.2d 495 (2d Cir. 1968).
3. *CT/East, Inc.* v. *Financial Services, Inc.,* 5 C.L.S.R. 817 (S.D.N.Y. 1975).

4. *See Wagner* v. *Graziano Construction Co.*, 136 A.2d 82 (1957).

5. *National Cash Register Co.* v. *Modern Transfer Co.*, 224 Pa. Super. Ct. 138, 302 A.2d 486, 5 C.L.S.R. 642 (1973).

6. *Lovable Co.* v. *Honeywell, Inc.*, 431 F.2d 668, 2 C.L.S.R. 690 (5th Cir. 1970).

7. *See R.C. Craig, Ltd.* v. *Ships of the Sea, Inc.*, 345 F. Supp. 1066 (S.D. Ga. 1972).

8. *See Neal-Cooper Grain Co.* v. *Texas Gulf Sulphur Co.*, 508 F.2d 283 (7th Cir. 1974).

9. *See Meyers* v. *Antone*, 227 A.2d 56 (D.C. 1967).

10. Equitable remedies, as opposed to monetary remedies, had their origin in the old English courts of equity, which were at one time separate and distinct from the courts of law.

11. *See Lenkay Sani Products Corp.* v. *Benitez*, 47 A.D.2d 524, 362 N.Y.S.2d 572 (1975).

12. *See United States* v. *Wegematic Corp.*, 360 F.2d 674 (2d Cir. 1966).

13. *See* U.C.C. §§ 2-102, 2-105.

14. *Lovable Co.* v. *Honeywell, Inc.*, op. cit.

15. Brandon, Dick H. *Data Processing Contracts: Structure, Content and Negotiations.* Cincinnati, Van Nostrand Reinhold, 1976. This is a difficult book to read, although there are many good example clauses which help make contract writing much easier.

16. *See Eberhard Manufacturing Co.* v. *Brown*, 61 Mich. App. 268, 232 N.W.2d 378 (1975).

17. *Hancock* v. *State*, 402 S.W.2d 906, 1 C.L.S.R. 562 (Tex. Crim. App. 1966).

18. The validity of these clauses is not questioned so long as there is reasonable nexus to the state chosen. *See Restatement (Second) Conflict of Laws*, § 187 (1971); and U.C.C. § 1-105. *See also* Rheinstein, Max. "Conflict of Laws in the Uniform Commercial Code," *Law and Contemporary Problems* 16:114-40, Winter-Spring 1951.

19. Bernacchi, Richard L., and Larsen, Gerald H. *Data Processing Contracts and the Law.* Boston, Little, Brown & Co., 1974. This excellent work provides extensive legal and technical footnotes.

20. *Clements Auto Co.* v. *Service Bureau Corp.*, 444 F.2d 169, 2 C.L.S.R. 143 (8th Cir. 1971).

ADDITIONAL REFERENCES

Bigelow, Robert, and Nycum, Susan. *Your Computer and the Law.* Englewood Cliffs, N.J., Prentice-Hall, 1975. This book is primarily designed for the data processing person, with one excellent chapter on contract negotiations.

Leutert, Werner W. "Project Management Games," *Datamation*, Sept. 15, 1970.

APPENDIX A

FANCY SYSTEMS
PROPOSAL

FOR THE INSTALLATION OF A FANCY SYSTEMS LIBRARY CIRCULATION CONTROL SYSTEM FOR THE CHAMBANA PUBLIC LIBRARY, CHAMBANA, ILLINOIS.

The Fancy Systems Company has developed a remarkable turnkey circulation system for libraries, which we call Fancicirc. It is an automated on-line inventory system which uses a stand-alone minicomputer. Transaction data are captured by a light pen reading device from bar-coded labels affixed to books and to borrower badges, or are keyed in at a keyboard/display terminal equipped with a cathode-ray tube screen. The keyboard/display terminal also allows on-line input to aid search of the inventory, patron and transaction files. All circulation terminals, computer equipment, computer programs and procedural manuals are supplied by Fancy Systems as a part of the total package.

The Fancicirc system proposed for the Chambana Public Library would be capable of handling the load carried by the library in its present stage, to wit:

20,000 registered borrowers using the system,
80,000 titles in the circulating collection data base,
125,000 items in the circulating collection data base, and
388,000 items issued annually from the library.

The Fancicirc system offers the following advantages over other systems on the market today:

1. Fancicirc is a complete system. There is no need to have any nearby large computer installation to print reports, nor is any long-distance data communications required.

2. Fancicirc is fully guaranteed to work. After all, it is not dependent on other installations; it is installed and operating in other libraries at this time (references will be supplied upon request); and the Fancy Systems Company is proud to stand behind its contractual obligations. We intend to build a reputation for serving libraries.

3. Since Fancy Systems supplies all the computer programs, a local library does not have to develop computer expertise.

4. Since the very same system is already working elsewhere, we can confidently say that we can install Fancicirc and make it fully operational within three months.

5. On-line systems are much more timely than batch systems. As such, you can catch a borrower with heavy fines pending while he is still trying to check out his next book, instead of the next day.

6. In the evening, after the library is closed, the system changes to batch format in order to generate notices, such as overdue notices and hold notices.

7. The transaction tapes generated by the system can be used to generate statistics, such as frequency of use by book, by type of borrower, etc. All you need to do is send the tapes to Fancy Systems headquarters, and we can run any report you desire, for a very nominal charge.

8. The most important feature, however, is the light pen itself. The borrower is checked out in no time. You have no badges which get jammed in the machine;

you don't have a flood of paper listing due dates; you simply stamp the book in the good old-fashioned way because you are sure that the computer has correctly checked out the book. No chance for error.

COMPONENTS

For the Chambana Public Library, the Fancicirc system best suited to its needs would have:

One Fancy CPU VI minicomputer, capable of handling the transactions with an average access time of 400 nanoseconds. It has a basic 16-bit instruction word and over 400 separate instructions. The basic system would include 131,323 bytes of memory and a 1566 byte cache memory.

One Fancidisc LP III disc storage unit, with room for four disc drives, which can be accessed in an average of 25 milliseconds. Peak transfer rate is in excess of 786,000 bytes per second.

One Fanciprint IV output printer, which is a 180 cps serial printer with a 256 byte buffer and 1200 baud EIA standard interface.

Three Fancy CRT III keyboard/display cathode ray tube terminals, which can display at a rate of 180 cps and which beeps when ready for the next entry.

Three Fancilight I light pen terminals, the latest in technology.

20,000 Fancibar Patron labels (bar-coded) and

125,000 Fancibar Book labels (bar-coded) to begin.

PROGRAM PACKAGES

The Chambana Public Library, with its present circulation policies of a 14-day checkout with one renewal and no reserve material, would be well suited to use the following packages in facilitating the operation of the components listed above:

The Fancipak circulation control program, developed by Fancy Systems, which allows input of the titles, with special designations for multiple copies, to correspond to numbers given on the respective bar-coded labels. Each book would have its own unique number. All users would also have unique numbers which are distinguishable from book numbers. The program would have three files:

Inventory — All titles are listed by title, author and corresponding book number, with annotation as to current status.

Patron — All patrons are listed with all relevant information, such as address, type of user, with a variable field available for entry of notes on fine and hold status, plus borrower number.

Transaction — Borrower number is linked to book number(s) with annotation as to type of transaction — check-out, hold, etc. Check-in drops the transaction from this file into the daily tape, which may be used for statistics or for a history of transaction.

The Fanciwrinkle batch processing program is used to generate overdue notices, recall notices, hold notices, bills for fines, and statistics by date. It is normally implemented when the library is closed because it supersedes access to the files from the Fancipak program.

TRAINING

The Fancy Systems Company believes that the Fancicirc turnkey circulation system is so user-oriented that the normal training needed for this system can be handled in an hour by the sales representative at the library itself. We do have courses available at the Fancy headquarters which are more intensive.

These courses would make the technical services librarian a skilled master of the system and make the changeover from your present manual circulation system to Fancicirc much easier. We think that with properly trained personnel, you will find the time needed to input the holding information surprisingly small.

Manuals are available for every step of the operation. We normally include enough for your operation as a matter of course.

PRICES

The following prices represent the latest in equipment, perfected just for you (and the many other satisfied users of the Fancicirc system). If, through the goodness of our subcontractors, our own costs in procuring the components should be lowered after the contract is signed, we will pass these savings on to you. Otherwise, all prices are firm if within three months of machine shipment.

Hardware Components	
Fancy CPU VI computer	$57,000
Fancidisc LP III storage unit	5,000
Fanciprint IV printer	700
3 Fancy CRT III terminals, at $4000	12,000
3 Fancilight I terminals, at $500	1,500
20,000 Fancibar Patron labels	
125,000 Fancibar Book labels	3,000
Wiring package	800
Program Packages	
Fancipak circulation control program	17,000
Fanciwrinkle batch processing report program, for use with Fancipak	3,000
TOTAL	$100,000

INSTALLATION DATE

Since so many potential customers are in the market for our system, we feel it necessary to warn you that you should sign up early for your own system. We can handle only so many installations per month, and the waiting list gets longer and longer. Presently, the Fancilight I terminals are about three months behind in delivery. Present estimates for delivery are set out below:

Contract signed:	Hardware:	Programs:	Fancilight I's:
April 25, 1977	Jan. 15, 1978	Jan. 20, 1978	April 10, 1978
May 9, 1977	Feb. 15, 1978	Feb. 22, 1978	April 30, 1978

APPENDIX B

FANCY SYSTEMS
PURCHASE AGREEMENT

PURCHASER:_____

The Purchaser agrees to purchase, and Fancy, by its acceptance of this Agreement, agrees to sell, on the following terms and conditions, the machines and features listed below and more fully described in the attached Specification Sheets.

The prices shown are FOB Fancy's plant. All transportation, rigging and draying charges will be paid by the Purchaser.

There shall be added to the prices shown below amounts equal to any taxes, however designated, levied or based on such prices or on this Agreement or the machines, including state and local privilege or excise taxes based on gross revenue, and any taxes or amounts in lieu thereof paid or payable by Fancy in respect of the foregoing, exclusive, however, of taxes based on net income. Any personal property taxes assessable on the machines after delivery to the carrier shall be borne by the Purchaser.

Terms

This Agreement must be received by Fancy on or before the Date of Installation of the machines. Payment in full for each machine shall be due upon the Date of Installation unless otherwise provided in an Installment Payment Agreement between Fancy and the Purchaser.

Date of Installation	Item No.	Type Model (Feature)	Warranty Category	Description	Quantity	Unit Price	Amount
						TOTAL	

Software (Program)	Product	Programming Classification	Testing Period	Date of Installation	Price
				TOTAL	

TOTAL OF MACHINE AND SOFTWARE PRODUCTS:

Site Preparation

1. The Purchaser shall prepare or cause to be prepared, at no expense to Fancy, a location or locations for the installation of the machines at its premises. Such location(s) shall be prepared in accordance with site preparation specifications provided by Fancy. The Purchaser shall advise Fancy when all required

preparations are completed, and with sufficient notice to permit a Fancy representative to inspect said installation location(s) at least one week prior to the scheduled date for the delivery of the machines. If, upon inspection, Fancy determines that the site preparation requirements have not been satisfied, Fancy may, at its option, reschedule delivery and installation to a mutually agreeable date, such date to be no later than one month after successful inspection of said installation location(s).

Delivery Schedule

2. The estimated delivery date is set forth in the description of machines and software in the Terms paragraph of this Agreement. In the event of delay or inability to deliver or install caused by any reason beyond Fancy's control, including, but not limited to, any delay or inability caused by subcontractors or suppliers, or by acts of God, fires, floods, wars, embargoes, labor disputes, acts of sabotage, riots, accidents, delays of carriers, voluntary or mandatory compliance with any government act, regulation, or request, Fancy may without penalty or liability, extend delivery and/or installation schedules to the earliest time deemed feasible by Fancy.

Installation

3. Fancy shall be responsible for the installation of the machines and shall connect the same to the power lines and any requisite safety switches which are installed by the Purchaser pursuant to paragraph 1 above. The Purchaser shall make all necessary arrangements to allow Fancy personnel access to the installation location(s) during normal business hours and at such other times as may be mutually agreed upon. If any special installation work must be performed or is required in order to comply with requirements of any governmental authority including, but not limited to, the procurement of special certificates, the same shall be performed and/or procured by the Purchaser at its expense. If any labor union or unions prevent Fancy from performing the work specified, the Purchaser shall make all required arrangements with the union or unions involved to permit Fancy to complete such work. Any additional cost related to labor disputes shall be borne by the Purchaser, and Fancy's obligation under such circumstances shall be limited to providing engineering supervision of installation and connection of the machines to existing wiring. Where applicable, Fancy shall connect the machines to telephone company-supplied data communication lines or equipment. Fancy shall be in no way responsible for the installation or the reliability of such telephone company-supplied lines or equipment.

Price Protection Period

4. Prices of the machines and software stated herein shall be subject to all established price increases except those increases which become effective during the three months immediately prior to the date of machine shipment. In the event that the price of any machine stated herein, or any software connected with such machine, is increased pursuant to the terms of this paragraph, the Purchaser may elect to terminate this Agreement as to that machine, or in its entirety. Purchaser may terminate that machine or the Agreement by writing to Fancy within 15 days of notification of the price increase; otherwise the higher prices shall be effective.

If Fancy's established price for any machine upon the Date of Installation or 45 days after plant shipment, whichever occurs first, shall be lower than the price for such machine stated in this Agreement, the Purchaser shall have the benefit of such lower price.

Warranty

5. Machines purchased under this Agreement may be either newly manufactured by Fancy from new and serviceable used parts which are equivalent to new in performance in these machines, or assembled by Fancy from serviceable used parts, or machines which have been previously installed. Machines assembled from serviceable used parts and machines previously installed will at the time of shipment meet product functional specifications currently applicable to new machines.

The Purchaser will be responsible for assuring the proper use, management and supervision of the machines and programs, audit controls, operating methods and office procedures, for establishing the necessary controls over access to data, and for establishing all proper check points and procedures necessary for the intended use of the machines and the security of the data stored therein. The Purchaser agrees that Fancy will not be liable for any damages caused by the Purchaser's failure to fulfill these responsibilities. The following Warranties shall apply to the machines described herein.

I. Service and Parts Warranty

Commencing on the Date of Installation, Fancy will maintain in good working order each Warranty Category A machine for one year and each Warranty Category B or C machine for three months, at no additional charge to the Purchaser. At the Purchaser's request, Fancy will make all necessary adjustments, repairs and parts replacements. All replacement parts will be new or equivalent to new in performance when used in these machines. All replaced parts will become the property of Fancy on an exchange basis. Fancy may, at its option, store maintenance equipment or parts on the Purchaser's premises that Fancy deems necessary to fulfill this Warranty.

Service pursuant to this Warranty as required at any time will normally be furnished by Fancy's nearest branch office or resident location. Fancy shall have full and free access to the machines to perform this service. There will be no charge for travel expense associated with warranty services except that actual expense shall be charged in those unusual instances where the site at which the machine is located is not normally accessible by private automobile or scheduled public transportation. The Purchaser shall promptly inform Fancy of any change in the machine location during the warranty period. Service outside the scope of this Warranty will be furnished at Fancy's applicable hourly rates and terms then in effect.

II. Parts Warranty

For one year commencing on the Date of Installation, Fancy warrants each Warranty Category B or C machine (excluding vacuum tubes and solid state and other electronic devices which are warranted for three months) to be free from defects in material and workmanship. Fancy's obligation is limited to furnishing on an exchange basis replacements for parts which have been promptly reported by the Purchaser as having been, in his opinion, defective and are so found by Fancy upon inspection. All replacement parts will be new or equivalent to new in performance when used in these machines. All replaced parts will become the property of Fancy on an exchange basis. No service will be furnished pursuant to this parts warranty.

III. Limitations

The foregoing warranties will not apply to repair of damage or increase in service time caused by: accident, transportation, neglect, or misuse; alterations (which shall include, but not be limited to, any deviation from circuit or structural machine design as provided by Fancy, installation or removal of Fancy features, or any other modification or maintenance related activities, whenever any of the foregoing are performed by other than Fancy representatives); any machine other than those owned by Fancy, under warranty provision of a Fancy purchase agreement or under a Fancy maintenance agreement; failure to provide a suitable installation environment with all facilities prescribed by the appropriate Fancy Installation Manual — Physical Planning (including but not limited to, failure of, or failure to provide adequate electrical power, air conditioning or humidity control); the use of supplies or materials not meeting Fancy specifications for such installation; or the use of the machine for other than data processing purposes for which designed.

Fancy shall not be responsible for failure to provide service or parts due to causes beyond its control or required to adjust or repair any machine or part if it would be impractical to do so because of alterations in the machine or its connection by mechanical or electrical means to another machine or device or if the machine is located outside the United States, Puerto Rico or the Canal Zone.

Limitation of Liability

FANCY MAKES NO REPRESENTATION OR WARRANTY OTHER THAN THAT SET FORTH IN THIS PURCHASE AGREEMENT. THE WARRANTY STATED HEREIN IS EXPRESSLY IN LIEU OF ALL OTHER WARRANTIES, EXPRESS OR IMPLIED, INCLUDING, BUT NOT LIMITED TO, ANY EXPRESS OR IMPLIED WARRANTY OF MERCHANTABILITY OR FITNESS FOR A PARTICULAR PURPOSE, OR AGAINST INFRINGEMENT.

The Purchaser further agrees that Fancy will not be liable for any lost profits, or for any claim or demand against the Purchaser by any other party.

No action, regardless of form, arising out of the transactions under this Agreement, may be brought by either party more than one year after the cause of action has accrued, except that an action for nonpayment may be brought within one year after the date of the last payment.

In no event will Fancy be liable for consequential damages even if Fancy has been advised of the possibility of such damages.

Title and Security Interest

6. Title to each machine passes to the Purchaser on the date of shipment from Fancy, or on the date of acceptance of this Agreement by Fancy, whichever is later. Fancy reserves a purchase money security interest in each of the machines listed herein in the amount of its purchase price. These interests will be satisfied by payment in full unless otherwise provided in an Installment Payment Agreement between Fancy and the Purchaser. A copy of this Agreement may be filed with appropriate state authorities at any time after signature by the Purchaser as a financing statement in order to perfect Fancy's security interest. Such filing does not constitute acceptance of this Agreement by Fancy.

Title to the Software shall not pass from Fancy to the Purchaser, and the software shall remain the sole property of Fancy at all times.

Fancy retains for itself all proprietary rights in and to all designs, engineering details, and other data pertaining to the machines and the software, and retains for itself the sole right to manufacture, lease, and sell any and all such machines and software. The software and the configuration of the machines shall be deemed trade secrets of Fancy.

Software License

7. Fancy hereby grants to the Purchaser a nonexclusive, nontransferable license to use the software in accordance with provisions of this paragraph. The software is furnished to the Purchaser only for use by the Purchaser with the machines listed in the Terms paragraph. The Purchaser shall not modify or copy the software or any portion thereof, and shall not provide or otherwise make available the software, or any portion thereof, in any form, to any third party without the prior written approval of Fancy. All of the software, including, but not limited to, operating systems, operating system components, and application programs, is and shall remain the sole property of Fancy.

Maintenance

8. Fancy shall provide, at the option of the Purchaser, an agreement for maintenance of the machines and software, covering parts, labor, and travel expenses for all corrective and preventive maintenance for a period of five (5) years. The performance by the Purchaser of its obligations hereunder shall be separate from and independent of the performance of either party of its obligations under such maintenance agreement.

Documentation

9. Fancy shall provide with the machines and software, without charge to the Purchaser (a) two copies of any manual written with respect to a particular machine listed in the Terms paragraph or two copies of any manual for several machines sold as a system listed in the Terms paragraph and (b) that number of Operator's Guides which is the same number of terminals listed in the Terms paragraph.

Training

10. Fancy shall provide, without charge to the Customer, group training sessions on the operation and use of the machines and software for up to three Purchaser personnel. Such sessions will be conducted for not more than ten days prior to and after the installation of the machines at times and at locations to be agreed upon by Fancy and the Purchaser. The Purchaser shall be responsible for the salaries and the travel and accommodation expenses of its personnel.

General Provisions

11. This Agreement is not assignable without written permission from Fancy; any attempt to assign any rights, duties or obligations which arise under this Agreement without such permission shall be void.

12. This Agreement will be governed by the laws of the State of Illinois. It constitutes the complete and exclusive statement of the agreement between the parties which supersedes all proposals, oral or written, and all other communications between the parties relating to the subject matter of this Agreement.

13. If any provision or provisions of this Agreement shall be held to be invalid, illegal or unenforceable, the validity, legality and enforceability of the remaining provisions shall not in any way be affected or impaired thereby.

14. This Agreement may only be changed in writing, executed on behalf of Fancy and of the Purchaser. The term "this Agreement" as used herein includes any applicable Installment Payment Agreement, Supplement, or future written amendment made in accordance herewith.

15. The Purchaser represents and warrants that he has read this Agreement, understands it, and agrees to be bound by its terms and conditions. The Purchaser further agrees that this Agreement is intended by the parties as a final, complete and exclusive statement of the terms of their agreement. No course of dealings between the parties and no usage of the trade shall be relevant to supplement any term used in this Agreement.

Received by Fancy at_____

                                                 Purchaser

by_____   by_____
        signature   signature

_____   _____
   name printed, title   name printed, title

on_____   on_____
           date   date

Accepted by Fancy by_____
                             signature, name printed, title

on_____
           date

APPENDIX C

VENDOR INSTRUCTIONS

In playing your role as vendors, you will need to come prepared to defend your company's financial position. The standard form contract you are using to begin discussion has been formatted by attorneys working for your firm in order to protect the firm at its weakest points. Although you do not want to lose the sale (you will make a $4000 bonus for it), you must try to get the purchaser to sign the contract with as little change as possible. If you change the contract too much, your manager may not accept it. (You can use that as an argument to the purchaser if you remember to connect that point with the "fact" that delay in signing means a longer wait for installation.) In order to give yourself an edge during the negotiations, present the contract already filled in, basing it on the proposal, but in the following manner:

Date of Installation	Type Model (Feature)	Warranty Category	Description	Quantity	Unit Price	Amount
1/20/78	Fancy CPU VI	A	mini-computer	1	$57,000	$57,000
1/20/78	Fancidisc LP III	A	storage unit	1	5,000	5,000
1/20/78	Fanciprint IV	C	printer	1	700	700
1/20/78	Fancy CRT III	B	CRT terminal	3	4,000	12,000
4/10/78	Fancilight I	B	light pen terminal	1	500	1,500
	Fancibar Patron labels	N/A		20,000	package price	
	Fancibar Book labels	N/A		125,000		3,000
1/20/78	DX 243	C	wiring package	1	800	800
					TOTAL	80,000

Software (Program) Product	Programming Classification	Testing Period	Date of Installation	Price
Fancipak circulation control	FX-5	N/A[1]	1/20/78	$17,000
Fanciwrinkle report	BXE-5	N/A[1]	1/20/78	3,000
			TOTAL	20,000

1. Plant tested.

Below I am listing some parameters to the bargaining situation that are only known by the vendors. These have to do with the company's internal structure. Whether you do well or not in your role-playing will depend on how well you protect the company's weak points. Remember, you don't want to go back to selling pocket calculators.

1. Notice the delivery dates. The actual truth is that there is only a 4-month delay presently, but your boss has directed you to give a late delivery schedule because he has hopes of selling a large university library and it would want preference. You can get leeway here, but if you give anything here, be sure to get other concessions in return.

2. Notice that there is no delivery date for the labels. Because of production control problems with the subcontractor, you are presently woefully behind in providing these. What you hope to do is to wait until just before installation to inform the purchaser. Then you will begin delivering them piecemeal.

3. Notice the warranty classifications. The truth is that there have been many serious problems in breakdowns with respect to the CRT and the printer. The printer is the worst offender. The truth, moreover, is that the sales department keeps that particular printer in this package simply to try to engender a taste in the purchaser for a maintenance contract after the warranty period expires. If the purchaser wants a better warranty for the printer, then try to get him to shift to a better printer. Offer him a Fanciprint VII at $1,500, with an A warranty category. If the purchaser wants to change the warranty category on the CRT, try to avoid it. You have no other CRT that is any better. You can make a false statement that the real problems for the CRT are in the wiring package. Since any real problems in the wiring package show up in the first couple of weeks, you can graciously offer to make it an A warranty category item.

4. Try to avoid putting the specifications listed in the proposal into the contract. You are hoping that the limitation of liability will keep those specifications out of the bargained agreement. The CPU actually has an average access time of 900 nanoseconds, but only in rare instances in the past has that been crucial. Since this is a small installation, you should have no problem, unless the purchaser has an exceptionally fast typist.

5. Examine the contract carefully and note the following tricks:

    a. New or "comparable" used equipment.

    b. Site preparation inspection. If your engineers come upon an unexpected delay later on, they can always have the inspector flunk the library's preparations in order to shift the blame for the delay. So keep that clause in there and the boys in the back will love you for it. (It has saved them their jobs in the past.)

    c. Try to avoid at all costs any inclusion of a clause giving penalty charges for delay in delivery, or make it inconsequential, i.e., for a very low dollar figure.

    d. Since Fancy owns the software, the tapes of the daily transactions are worthless on their own unless provision is made by the purchaser for a translating program which could make the tapes usable elsewhere. Be careful. You want to keep the purchaser technically naïve so he will be stuck with you for life. ("Life" is another way of saying job tenure.)

    e. There are subtle differences between what the proposal says with respect to documentation and training and what the contract offers.

6. Avoid testing on site. Also try to keep your own personnel in charge of testing. Again, stress your technical superiority, and neglect the fact that any moderately intelligent librarian should be able to decide whether a system works or not.

7. Remember that the company's basic strength is in making timely deliveries and its basic weakness is breakdown in the peripherals. At least, this week, that is.

RICHARD W. BOSS
University Librarian
Princeton University
Princeton, New Jersey

Negotiating an Automated Circulation System: The Librarian's Viewpoint

I THINK THAT IT was my experience in a contracts course in law school that convinced me that I should not be a lawyer, but since then I've found that no librarian's work today is entirely free of legal problems. This is just one of the increasing complexities of librarianship that make it challenging and enjoyable.

I'm not sure that my courses in law school increased my ability to negotiate for a circulation system. That was confirmed to me when, in preparation for this speech today, I looked at the last contract that we negotiated. In rereading it only a matter of months later, many of the provisions in it seem naïve. In the final analysis, it comes down to the fact that no contract can offer absolute protection in all circumstances.

Let me start with a little history about why, when and how we undertook the automation of the circulation system at the Princeton University Library. In 1975 the library operated with a 2-card, manual circulation system that was not satisfactory. There were people in the front filing and retrieving cards by call number and people (four FTE) in the back room filing and retrieving another copy of that circulation card by patron's name in order to respond to queries from the Controller's Office about outstanding commitments by those leaving the university. As in many university libraries, there was also a pattern of very heavy demand on circulation during the ten or fifteen minutes before a class change. Approximately one-third or more of all circulations occurred in that slightly more than 10-minute period each hour. We were unable to put enough people out front to take care of everyone and still provide optimum service. Another consideration was the need for better statistical data to aid in decisions on transferring materials to Princeton's storage library about three miles from the main building, selecting materials, and pinpointing locations for shelf reading.

I will digress momentarily to describe a project that was very important, but somewhat frustrating. Princeton's open stacks library has a high level of collection utilization, but has been choking on its own success. Random sampling demonstrated that about 132,000 of 2 million volumes were out of place on the shelves in the main library building. There seemed to be no way to commit enough staff to continue full shelf reading on a regular basis. This made it desirable to concentrate effort where there was greatest activity; however, the manual circulation system did not give an adequate indication of where that activity was. Elaborate samplings were taken several times, and it was discovered that in some areas the shelves were out of order at twenty times the average rate. This made it very important to determine where the activity was concentrated in order to put the necessary efforts into the appropriate areas. The rate at which the disorder occurred in the stacks had a high correlation to the circulation patterns; however, circulation patterns themselves change constantly throughout the academic calendar, depending on what readings are assigned.

In the fall of 1975 we began to examine the alternatives. The systems analyst, the circulation librarian and I made brief visits to about twenty libraries using seven different circulation systems. This was done to give us an idea of what was currently available and a sense of how those users felt about the companies that had supplied their hardware and software. We narrowed the field to three prospects: two existing systems and one in development. A somewhat larger committee was then appointed to conduct a more exhaustive evaluation of the three main prospects. That committee was chaired by a new staff member who had been involved in the installation of an automated circulation system at another major institution. Also included on the committee was the circulation librarian, the reserve librarian (because of the immediate need to extend the circulation system to the reserve book division where many of our circulation problems were), a representative from Technical Services, and the engineering librarian, who represented branch libraries because we were interested in the potential extension of the system outside the main building. Princeton has 4 branch libraries with circulations of over 50,000 a year; 3 of these have collections in excess of 100,000 volumes. There seemed to be a real potential for decentralizing the system.

The automation committee undertook a detailed evaluation, visiting various installations and talking with those who had experience with the companies involved. The more places they went, the more conflicting were the reports they got — which prompted them to look even further. This points out the undesirability of seeking the opinion of only one library. In many cases those reports were based on misunderstandings of fact. The committee attempted to qualify the systems on the basis of their technical and functional attributes and recommended two systems. One vendor offered an established product. The other system, however, offered greater potential, not only in terms of making innovations in the statistical area, but also in the prospect of addressing our reserve requirements in a much shorter time frame. It was a calculated gamble in the case of the second vendor, as there would have to be a substantial time commitment by the library staff.

When the committee had made its recommendations, negotiation began with one of the two companies. We took, at that point, the more conservative posture because there was some opposition to automation. This decision was based on the meeting of the Library Council, discussion with the purchasing agent, and our legal counsel. Contract negotiation proved to be very complex. There were some points about which we felt strongly and yet could not get revised to meet our unique requirements. We therefore obtained a copy of a standard contract from the other vendor and began discussion of contract terms with them. The contract terms, drawn from various versions of the contracts of both of those companies, make up the major portion of this paper.

We had two underlying concerns as we undertook contract negotiation. Our first concern was dependability. There were reports of failure to perform, unfulfilled promises of delivery and late delivery. We wanted dependability — to ensure it somehow through contract negotiations. The second concern was to avoid hidden costs. The budget was finite, almost inflexible, so there could be no surprises in terms of dollars and cents.

The first specific contract provision to concern us was the description. What exactly was to be included? The hardware portion is obviously the more specific. It itemizes a central processing unit, the terminal controller, certain terminals of specified numbers and types. However, this constitutes only about 40 percent of the value of the system. Of more importance is the software. What software packages are actually included? Care is needed here as this is a double-edged sword. If one gets too detailed in itemizing everything that one could think of, one is much more likely to be hurt by what one failed to request. Broad, general phrases are better in terms of future specific software requirements. We incorporated the standard descriptions that appeared in the promotional literature of the companies into the contract, by reference in one case and itemization in another.

The second concern was the matter of delivery date and liability for nondelivery or late delivery. After contacting about one-third of all the on-line circulation systems users in the country by telephone or in person during the course of our efforts, we found that delivery was such a widespread problem that it was necessary to include it. During the early negotiations we were very insistent on penalty clauses for late delivery and, in fact, did two versions of the contract with penalty clauses stipulating x hundreds of dollars per month for late delivery.

Our attitudes shifted during the negotiation process — away from concerns about delivery toward concerns about acceptance. Anyone can put the hardware on the loading dock and the software in your cabinet, but the real question is whether the operating circulation system can check books in and out satisfactorily and perform other operations of circulation. Thus, the acceptance clause became a much greater object of concern as we matured in the contract negotiation process.

A third concern was that of risk of loss or damage. When does the obligation or the liability transfer? Does it transfer at time of shipment? At time of receipt? This is perhaps of minor importance in working with most companies because of insurance provisions; nevertheless, we specified in the contract that liability be transferred to the library at time of delivery.

The next concern was that of site preparation. Whose responsibility is it? This is generally spelled out in a boiler plate which would be provided by a vendor. Site specifications are usually mentioned in a contract. In this particular case, we were naïve. We didn't pay much attention to this, because we had contacted a large number of institutions and asked how much installation costs had been. They very specifically ranged from $3000 to $5000, so we incorporated that into our planning and paid little more attention to it. Little did we realize that due to shortcomings of our 1948 building we could have either all heat or all cooling, but no mixing during the transition periods of the year. In the fall and spring, the temperature can be unbearable. Those circumstances can cause serious problems with the central processor. Moreover, the system could not be modified simply by putting in supplementary cooling facilities because local building codes prohibited window units. Site preparation costs subsequently totaled more than $13,000. This, of course, violated our "no hidden or unexpected costs" concern with which we began negotiation. Were we to do it over again, we would not necessarily make this a matter of contract, but we would certainly arrange for an inspection and evaluation by the vendor and some fairly specific cost estimates by a local contractor to determine what would actually be involved in site preparation and installation.

The fifth concern was terms of payment. Contract provisions vary: one contract stipulated 30 percent payment at time of order, 50 percent more on delivery and 20 percent on acceptance. In other words, the vendor would have 80 percent of the money at the time of delivery. This provision offended us. We didn't want to pay for the system until it was working. While appreciating the cash flow requirements of the vendor, we didn't feel very businesslike in paying the 80 percent, which would not only cover the vendor's costs of hardware, but probably most of the software as well. After considerable negotiation with the vendors we were able to have this provision changed.

The next area was that of training. This may be very important if the system is a new one. The vendor may stipulate that training is available to six people for up to ten days preceding or following the installation. For a well-established system, such a training clause may be satisfactory. However, if the system is relatively new, it is highly unlikely that training could be performed in such a short time. Our concern was for a training clause that best reflected the particular nature of our installation.

Warranty was the next issue, and it proved to be a very difficult area. One vendor's contract read: "*X* warrants only that the system shall be free from defects in material and workmanship at the time of delivery and for a period of 30 days thereafter. *X*'s liability under this warranty is limited to the repair and replacement FOB factory at *X*'s option and expense of any defective or nonconforming product." A warranty on the parts and labor for thirty days on something as complex as an automated system was unsatisfactory, especially since the acceptance test would probably not even be conducted within the warranty period. We wanted a warranty that said that it was fit for the purpose, i.e., for circulating books. If it didn't circulate books we wanted the ability to make a claim under the warranty. That is not very easily done. In fact, we were unable to get a warranty of fitness for purpose from any vendor and found that the compromise solution was to modify the acceptance test. It seemed that the acceptance test would have to be the critical nucleus of the whole contract.

The next concern was that of limitation of liability. One version of a vendor's contract stipulated that their liability did not exceed the total amount paid to the company. We felt that if a problem arose due to faulty installation or equipment and as a result someone were seriously harmed, a multimillion dollar suit could result, and we did not want to be in a situation where the vendor's liability was limited to the amount of the payment we had made. Renegotiation removed the limitation, but we were unable to avoid a series of restricting clauses concerning the circumstances under which there would be liability. There was also a one-year limitation clause in almost every contract we saw, so that legal recourse was available for only one year after purchase. We refused to accept that one-year restriction and were successful in renegotiating the contract.

Virtually every vendor-written contract begins with a fairly standard boiler plate. If one expresses concern about specific clauses, the response usually is, "Well, just about everybody who does business with us signs this contract." This is not merely salesmanship; the vast majority of librarians we spoke to had accepted the standard contract submitted by the company without effort at extensive, serious review.

The next item was the matter of acceptance. There were different versions of the acceptance test. One that initially looked very appealing called for a demonstration of the system at a time to be determined by the vendor, but within a certain number of specified days after installation. It listed a series of twenty-seven steps that would be demonstrated only once. If the system went through the twenty-seven steps successfully, it would be considered acceptable. Because the list was fairly exhaustive, including almost every conceivable function a circulation system could perform, we were duly impressed. However, another institution's acceptance document made us realize that our real concern was continuity of performance. Thus, we sought instead to negotiate a provision that the system perform as spelled out in the contract appendix for a period of thirty consecutive days at a level of 90 percent efficiency. If a single terminal were out or a single function were not performed satisfactorily, it would constitute down time and if that aggregated to more than 10 percent, the system would not be acceptable. Failing the first 30 days, a second 30-day period would ensue, then another; after 120 days we would have the option of either requesting a replacement of the system or having the system removed. Also, payment was made contingent upon acceptance. The matter of acceptance is particularly critical if the vendor has in the past made prompt delivery but has failed to have the system operational within a reasonable period of time after delivery, or if the vendor is new and has no history of performance.

If we were to enter contract negotiations again, we would commit much more attention to the acceptance clause. In every version of the contract of every company with which we talked, we failed to differentiate adequately between satisfactory and unsatisfactory performance of a function. That a system will register a patron or check in a book is not necessarily meaningful if the function is performed very, very slowly. Many of you are acquainted with OCLC and know the problems of response time. Frankly, our contract contained no protection against this problem.

Maintenance was the next issue addressed. The maintenance fee is generally waived for the first year after installation. Although prepared to pay for this in subsequent years, we wanted assurance that maintenance costs would not get out of hand. Maintenance costs $15,000-20,000 per year on a sophisticated system and we wanted to prevent those costs from rising very dramatically. We attempted to protect ourselves by including an escalator clause that set limitations on price increases.

The next issue was the ability to utilize new releases. There is, of course, a serious economic pressure to standardize. A vendor installing a number of systems will increasingly seek to standardize that system so that development costs can be borne by a larger number of users. If our system became more and more standardized after installation, we wanted to be able to utilize the new releases. That "utilizability" clause was very important to us because we had encountered libraries that had installed early versions of a system and then had considerable difficulty adapting to the standardized system that subsequently developed.

Our next concern was that of escrow of software. What if the vendor went bankrupt or dropped production? One extremely small vendor might cease doing business — and then? Another, very large company might nonetheless decide to drop the line because of poor return on investment. We wanted to be assured that under those circumstances we would have access to the software and be able to continue the development of the system on our own. An escrow agreement became an important element of the contracts negotiated with two firms.

The next item of concern was the right of resale. One contract specified that we had no right of resale. We wondered what their reasons were. Why did they take that position? This is a very important question to ask in the negotiating process. The underlying concern was that the vendor did not want the software to fall into the hands of a competitor. We solved that problem by having the vendor grant right of resale of hardware to anyone and limit right of resale of the software to those not engaged in the business of selling or servicing automated circulation systems.

This type of discussion was at the heart of all the changes mentioned. In fact, my own view of the contract now is that it is the record of a series of discussions and agreements that have been reached. In the final analysis, one must have faith in the other party because there is no way to anticipate every conceivable circumstance against which one might wish to be protected. A very tightly drawn contract can work against, as well as for, the parties, because it limits what one can get as well as setting a limit to what one may have to give. For that reason it is important to maintain a feeling of confidence and trust throughout the negotiating process. Any feeling that the vendor is not trustworthy or reliable is a good reason to get out of that negotiation. Sticking with it and thinking that the boiler plate in the contract will somehow provide protection is a mistake.

My last comment is made on the basis of admittedly very limited experience: one really has to know what one wants before going into negotiations. There has to be a great deal of homework. This is best done by visiting a lot of libraries, talking with many librarians, and finding out what problems they had. This should help both to avoid repeating those problems and in working with the vendor when and if problems do arise.

QUESTION AND ANSWER PERIOD

What role do attorneys play?

All three companies with whom we discussed contract terms presented us, at one point or another, with a fairly standard document which had obviously been prepared by an attorney. We reacted to it from the standpoint of its functional aspects — how it dealt with our specific requirements. We then submitted these reactions to our attorney, explained what we wanted to accomplish, and asked if the contract terms really reflected our needs and how we should state some of our requirements that were missing. The attorney phrased the appropriate legal language which we passed on to the vendor. They in turn referred it to their attorneys.

One difficulty we ran into was that after quickly reaching an understanding between the top people in the vendor's company and the top people in the university, both would refer the idea of that agreement to their respective attorneys; but when it came back in legal language, we all felt somehow that we were being more restricted than we had intended. It seemed that legal counsel on both sides was far more conservative and protective of their party's interests than the parties themselves seemed to want. It was difficult enough understanding the legal position of our attorney, much less that of the attorney for the vendor. In a few cases we actually had to request our attorney to leave out the verbiage, and keep the concept simple. This is not, however, an indictment of all attorneys. In this case, the attorney's problems were very much a reflection of his own inexperience in dealing with this particular kind of contract. Our attorney attempted to protect not only us but himself as well by putting in a great deal of additional language. I've wondered since then if it would have been better to seek assistance from someone who had a reputation for knowing the ins and outs of electronics contracts and automated systems contracts. However, as our attorney became educated, we also became educated and those problems began to disappear.

How experienced were the vendors?

To my knowledge, one vendor had already negotiated more than 100 contracts for an automated circulation system before ours. For the other vendor, our contract was probably their first, or one of the very first.

Were you concerned about the broad general terms of the contract you finally signed?

The vendors were already speaking in very broad terms because they didn't have a system already packaged and ready for delivery. It made one want to be more careful in the contract. On the other hand, this also left open the possibility of resolving some of the problems we had seen in existing systems, which was an exciting prospect. There was also the hope that we might formulate some innovative solutions. As a result of the negotiations back and forth, trust developed and we were prepared to take risks on the side of greater generality. Some of our very specifically phrased demands began to disappear. For example, the penalty clauses were removed in the late stages of the negotiation. Both of us wanted to install a good working system — the vendor wanted it because it had a reputation at stake in terms of future contracts with libraries, and we wanted it because we had a reputation at stake in terms of our student body and faculty.

What did you do when you reached an impasse?

We reached impasse with both of the vendors with whom we dealt. Usually those situations were resolved by changing the cast of characters. An impasse is a product of the people involved, as well as of the organizations. By sending in a different individual who would approach the problem from a slightly different perspective, it was possible to resolve matters. Even where we didn't actually get our way, we did at least get an understanding of what the other was trying to protect. There's obviously a risk for the library, but there's also a risk for the vendor. It is, of course, the understanding of the respective risks that makes it possible to reach a compromise.

What kind of escrow agreement was developed?

The following excerpts will give an idea: "*X* shall deposit in escrow, in a depository located in the state of New Jersey, a copy of the current version of all software, proprietary or otherwise, which are essential to support the system. Software deposited by *X* in compliance with this provision are listed in paragraph G below. Upon the moment of deposit with the escrow depository, the purchaser shall have a nontransferable nonexclusive license to use the software deposited in connection with the system associated with this contract." A definition of software appeared in the next paragraph, and in the following paragraph the circumstances in which there would be access to the software were spelled out. Such circumstances include insolvency, bankruptcy of the supplier, phasing-out of production and/or sale of the system, inability to provide maintenance services for the system, or inability to develop software improvements which keep abreast of technological advances in the library systems industry. Immediately upon the occurrence of any of the foregoing, full right of access to the materials deposited in escrow shall belong to the purchaser. Escrow is basically the designation of a place (i.e., a bank), the spelling out of what shall be there, and the statement of circumstances under which access by the purchaser shall be valid.

Why didn't you specify that acceptance would be subject to your being satisfied?

Frankly, we thought there might be circumstances where certain vendors might want our account badly enough to write in such a clause. However, we had mixed feelings about that kind of requirement. We doubted whether such a provision would hold up in court, because the court would somehow have to determine the reasonableness of the standard of satisfaction. We sought rather to have a provision that spelled out to both parties at what point the system would be considered successful. The contract is really nothing more than a summary of mutual agreements.

Since there are many parties involved, both during negotiation and times later when problems may arise, common understanding must exist among the circulation librarian, reserve librarian, systems analyst, head librarian, university purchasing agency and several others on the staff. Simply to request satisfaction creates difficulties in pinpointing *whose* satisfaction. If at any one time our people had been polled, very different attitudes about the degree of our success would surface. The provisions in the acceptance test are depersonalized and therefore less subject to in-house disagreement.

Did you spend a lot of time on the maintenance agreement?

The contract contains a maintenance clause that has a standard maintenance agreement associated with it. We did not commit the same amount of care to review of the standard maintenance agreement that we did to the main contract, primarily because we didn't object to any of the maintenance contracts submitted by the vendors.

You'll have to live with the maintenance agreement for several years. Why do you feel you came out okay?

The point is very well taken; it is a poor reflection on us for not having put much emphasis on the maintenance agreement. However, it is a positive reflection on the vendor with whom we ultimately signed that the standard maintenance agreement (which was actually developed for another product of the same company), is clear and comprehensive. It has obviously withstood several years of revision in a way that the circulation system contract has not.

How long did the entire process take?

In October or November 1975 we began to investigate our alternatives and it only took about a month to narrow seven systems to three. It then took the committee three or four months to make its recommendation. Contract negotiations with two companies lasted approximately four months. The contract terms which took the most time were payment, warranty, acceptance, the utilizability of new releases, escrow of software and the right of resale. Those particular items were the only ones which required more than one exchange. It was primarily the reconciliation of the verbal agreement with the actual documents that constituted the most time-consuming element. After the contracts were drawn, it took several months for delivery. Thus, it was a little over one year.

You're fortunate in not having a state purchasing office, aren't you?

That is true; our situation is unusual in that we are a private institution and, therefore, have very few bidding requirements imposed on us. We do, however, have close supervision by a campus purchasing agent who makes certain that the university's interests are well served. We must demonstrate that we have investigated the alternatives and explain why we have chosen a certain alternative. We had several sessions during which we presented justification to the purchasing agent that, even though it was the library's money, the university's interests were properly served. Had we been using general university funds, the constraints would have been much greater.

How were you yourself involved?

I was involved at three times. The first was at the very beginning, in pinpointing the seven systems and narrowing them to three. This happened simply because I was the only one who had then had prior experience with automated circulation systems. The second stage of my involvement was when the committee made a recommendation to the Library Council, the chief policy-making body of the library. Because the recommendation was a conditional one, there had to be several meetings in order to get an understanding of the caveats involved. After all of the functional and technical requirements had been substantially resolved and it came to questions of warranty, payment, acceptance, utilizability and escrow of software, I then became the chief spokesperson for the university. Although this was the role of the purchasing agent, it seemed more important to have someone who had the best combination of knowledge of the system as well as the university's purchasing requirements.

What has actually been installed?

The system has been installed in the Circulation Division of Firestone Library and is scheduled to be installed in the Reserve Book Division during the next few weeks. We are behind the projected schedule for three reasons: slow delivery of components from subcontractors, problems with site preparation (primarily the air conditioning), and some difficulties in the performance of the system which only recently was traced to a hardware failure.

At this point, I'm not the least bit concerned about the system passing a test on a particular day; however, I'm very much concerned with it performing well over a long period of time. The acceptance test will probably occur this summer, which will be within six months of the arrival of the first components on our loading dock.

G.E. GURR
Manager, Library Systems
3M Company
St. Paul, Minnesota

Negotiating a Turnkey System: The Vendor's Viewpoint

MY TALK TODAY WILL be from the viewpoint of a business manager responsible for product development, product marketing and product service, while at the same time meeting established goals for profitability. It is not my intention to give a highly technical or legalistic presentation. First, I am not qualified to do so, and second, you are more likely to benefit from understanding the general concepts involved in contracting and leaving the legal details to counsel.

Before I begin my talk I would like to digress for a few moments on the subject of profits and the free enterprise system. In order to understand the vendor's position in a negotiation it is important to understand the framework within which he operates.

3M Company is a collection of little businesses that are connected. Library Systems is one of those businesses and, like the others, is identified as a profit center. Profits are regarded by some as antisocial, but they are in fact essential to the functioning of individual firms and of the entire economy. Money is invested in a publicly held company like 3M by private individuals and by other companies. They risk their investment in the hope of a return better than that available from safer investments, such as putting the money in a bank or buying government bonds. The corporation risks that investment money by doing research, developing new products, building new plants to produce those products, and hiring more people to sell those products.

Forty-eight percent of pretax profits go to the federal government for corporate taxes. Obviously, some part of that tax is then redistributed for various social purposes, including the funding of libraries. Approximately one-half the remaining 52 percent is distributed to the stockholders, the investors who risked their money initially. This dividend is one of the incentives that causes millions of individuals to provide the capital needed to keep this country going. The remaining part of the profit is used to build new plants, hire people and develop products needed by customers. Obviously, without profits a business cannot continue long, nor even continue to support equipment or systems previously sold to customers.

Library Systems is a profit center within the 3M Company organization; that is, 3M keeps track of the expenses and income of its Library Systems unit as a separate entity. That entity is expected to contribute profits to the corporation and to show growth from year to year, and is judged on how well it succeeds. The business entity and its manager are judged upon growth in sales and growth in profits.

As a unit within a very large corporation, Library Systems naturally has many corporate resources on which to draw. For example, there is a fine staff of lawyers who can provide counsel on contractual matters but who charge their services back to the operating units. This expense becomes part of the ongoing operating expense of each profit center and must be recovered as part of the income generated from sales. There are no free lunches. This should help to clarify why a vendor must make a profit by selling products and services. Profits are a necessary element of a vendor's ability to continue in business and to provide after-sales support.

In discussing negotiation from the corporate viewpoint, there are several points to consider: the general philosophy of negotiation, some of the vendor's concerns, some of the more common problems encountered in drafting contracts, some thoughts on what should be considered elements of the contract, what to do if performance of the contract does not go according to plan, and a little more philosophy in closing.

NEGOTIATION PHILOSOPHY

Basic to a satisfactory negotiation of a contract is a meeting between the two parties in good faith and trust with full disclosure of the facts from both sides, and a willingness to negotiate. In other words, there must be a willingness to listen to the other party, and a willingness to give as well as take. Both sides must be open with each other. This does not mean that there cannot be some plan of negotiation on each side, with some points that won't be negotiated and others that will be waived. However, important facts should not be concealed if the negotiation is to work.

An enormous amount of time, money and energy is wasted each year by parties that should never have reached the negotiation stage in their discussions. On one hand, it is a waste for a prospective purchaser to enter negotiations with a supplier if the purchaser does not have or cannot get the funding required for the purchase. On the other hand, it is senseless for a supplier to negotiate with a prospective purchaser if he does not have a product that suits the user's needs. These two elements are necessary for any constructive negotiation to begin: the ability to purchase and the ability to supply.

At the end of the negotiation when agreement is reached, it is important that the agreement be reduced to writing. If this cannot be done, then the negotiations have failed. The contract document should incorporate the understanding reached by the two parties. It may appear that there is a conflict between creating an atmosphere of trust while at the same time preparing a careful documentation of the understanding reached. This is not so. The contract is not a weapon to be used against an adversary; it is a tool to avoid misunderstanding.

A third equally necessary but less tangible element in negotiation is a relationship of trust and good faith between the parties. It is senseless to negotiate with a contractor to build a home if there is a good chance the builder will go bankrupt.

If a contractor built ten houses and all of them have been shoddily constructed, why should the eleventh be different, no matter what the contract specifications call for? If the salesman trying to sell a used Cadillac is shifty and evasive in answering questions about the history of the automobile, it would only be natural to be cautious.

Similarly, in professional relationships with vendors, questions should be answered directly and accurately and requests for references met. Vendors should receive the same treatment from the purchasers.

If you need a bicycle to get from home to work (one-half mile away) it makes no sense to negotiate the price of a used Greyhound bus because you think you can buy one cheaply. If you need to haul your son's high school hockey team to games each week, there's no sense economizing by negotiating on the price of a motorcycle with sidecar.

In both cases your needs will not be satisfied. In the one case the product is too much for your needs, in the other too little. These examples are absurd, but then so are some of the real-world situations that I see each year. (As an aside, I would comment that it is far more usual to request more than is needed than less.)

A successful contract negotiation will result in terms and conditions to which both sides can adhere. A seller will be looking for a fair return on his investment, and the buyer should be looking for the lowest fair price, not necessarily the lowest price.

I frequently deal with supplier companies, some of which are quite small. During contract negotiations it is not unusual to have to ask a supplier whether the prices quoted are actually high enough to cover costs adequately. An error in judgment can work a great hardship on a company and will usually result in its becoming a less than satisfactory vendor. Unusual cost situations, such as a sudden increase in the price of a raw material, may necessitate modifying a contract to allow for a corresponding price increase.

Why should we have these concerns for the other person's point of view as well as our own? 3M has been in business for seventy-five years and plans to be around for many years to come. Thus, it is necessary to consider the point of view of others as well as 3M Company's own. Developing a good relationship with a supplier increases our ability to rely on him. We don't want a supplier to let us down in the middle of a critical job or to drag his feet, unwilling to go the extra mile because of the financial loss he is already taking as a result of contract terms. Furthermore, costs must be properly segregated, i.e., in the right place. A supplier losing money on one job will naturally plan to make it up on the next one — which means the next time we deal with him our costs will be distorted, probably in a way we hadn't projected. This in turn can result in selling prices being distorted in the marketplace compared with what they might have been, and perhaps compared with our competition. Why don't we try to put the screws to the supplier and let him make it up in his dealings with others? Again, the answer is the same: orderliness, continuity, predictability, etc. Why should a supplier continue to work with us if he can find other people who will treat him better? We would then have to go through the learning curve all over again with a different company.

It would be wrong to get the impression that 3M is a big pushover for any request, no matter how unreasonable. However, it is very important to 3M that both negotiating parties come out with a contract that benefits each of them. More generous contract terms cost the user in some way.

I don't personally consider the Golden Rule to be an absolute truth; however, from a pragmatic point of view, it is the only way to operate. There is no way to be certain of getting fair treatment from others, but treating them fairly gives the best chance. It is simply good sense from a self-serving viewpoint. With this in mind, let me turn now to some of the concerns of the vendor.

THE VENDOR'S CONCERN

Probably the first concern of the vendor is to know and have documented exactly what is expected of him. Goods and services can then be priced in order to make a reasonable profit. Any vagueness or uncertainty, any expansion or increase in the scope of requirements must result in an increase in price, for it will certainly increase the vendor's cost.

Another major concern of the vendor is that after the vendor accepts a contract, the purchaser may take an unreasonable position in expecting more than the vendor had agreed to supply. This could happen for a number of reasons:

1. The two parties did not really understand each other's position in the first place.
2. The purchaser changed his mind.
3. The purchaser's needs changed.
4. New capabilities are developed.
5. The buyer is flighty or irrational.

It is for these reasons that the vendor is likely to be extremely reluctant to warrant fitness for purpose. He should have no reluctance in warranting compliance with his own published specifications or in the specifications of a contract that he has signed. From the vendor's point of view, fitness for purpose is a serious problem because purpose is normally not documented, but exists only in the mind of the purchaser. This causes the definition of purpose to keep changing.

COMMON STUMBLING BLOCKS

Purchasing Agent Role

The purchasing agent often creates difficulty in arriving at a satisfactory contract. He is usually a very busy, overworked individual. He would like to do things in the routine way, the way approved by the system within which he works. Adherence to the routine minimizes the time and effort spent in recognizing and reconciling the needs of both parties.

When a formula has been developed that gives the agent the protection he wants, he may be extremely reluctant to take the time to use a modified approach. The individual purchasing agent finds it much easier to go with the system than to try to modify provisions to state the concepts to which the parties have agreed.

Often an understanding is reached between the librarian and the vendor about the general terms and conditions that are suitable, but the contract details are then turned over to the purchasing agent who until that time has had no involvement in the discussions. Ideally, the counsel and purchasing agent should be involved before turning over a draft contract to them. If nothing else, it is simply a matter of courtesy to advise them of the upcoming need for their assistance so they may plan it in their schedules. More important, though, is that when their help is needed they will already be familiar with the terms and will not have to go through a time-consuming updating process.

State Codes

From the vendor's viewpoint, the great variability from state to state of purchasing procedures, required provisions, forbidden provisions, etc. creates an enormous work load. Many organizations, including the American Bar Association, recognize this problem. The ABA has drafted a proposed Uniform Procurement Code which is under consideration in many states. Some day it may be adopted as was the Uniform Commercial Code; when it is, it will greatly simplify contracting. At the moment, what one state demands might be absolutely forbidden by another. The vendor is usually somewhat flexible and willing to negotiate, but sometimes the state is not.

Applicable Laws

Often the final clause of a contract will state that the document includes all of the agreement between the two parties. However, this can leave ambiguous whether agreement has been reached that items not addressed by the contract are governed by provisions of the appropriate law (e.g., the Uniform Commercial Code), or whether this statement merely indicates that the items have not been discussed or negotiated.

Uniform Commercial Code

It is important to realize that the provisions of the Uniform Commercial Code (UCC) govern contracts for the sale of goods but not services. The UCC allows some of its provisions to be modified by the parties; others cannot be modified, even if both parties try to do so. Where it is appropriate, these modifications should be made part of the contract. For example, the "fitness for purpose" concept for computer systems is one which is at best difficult to apply, even though this concept is a part of the UCC provisions.

Limits of Responsibility

The vendor will naturally attempt to define the limits of his responsibility. If he cannot satisfactorily do so, it should be expected that he will charge more to cover the extra risk that he is absorbing. Of course, if he feels that the risk he is being asked to assume is totally unreasonable, then he should not enter into the contract.

Indemnification

Most contracts contain language which indemnifies and holds the buyer harmless from loss or injury (personal or property) which occurs during the performance of the contract, whether it is caused by the negligence of the vendor, third parties, or even the buyer. Frequently, however, there is a difference of opinion as to the way in which this intention is expressed. In fact, a number of judgments have given opposite interpretations of the meaning of virtually the same language, even by courts in the same state. Usually the point of contention is whether the contractor should be held liable for damage resulting from sole negligence of the buyer. This is unreasonable, and it is in fact held to be against public policy in a number of states. The buyer should have insurance to cover himself against his own negligent actions. Moreover, the contract should specifically state that the contractor is not liable for loss or damage resulting from sole negligence of the buyer. 3M's position as a vendor on indemnification is to be "reasonable" in the legal sense. 3M prefers to accept responsibility for its own negligence in the areas where it has responsibilities. This then defers resolution of any situation of conflict involving damages to common law.

The library's insistence that the vendor accept all responsibility (whether for damage done by the library or not) has several harmful effects. First, costs will increase — and the purchase price will have to be increased to reflect these increased costs. Secondly, from a long-term viewpoint, there will be serious social consequences. Insurance costs will increase. Many companies will eventually be unable to get insurance. This could even lead to the total destruction of small and even medium-sized companies that are unable to insure themselves and would thus have a serious impact on the entire free enterprise system.

Liquidated Damages

Another common stumbling block is the subject of liquidated damages. If it is recognized in advance that it would be extremely difficult or impossible to assess the amount of damages resulting from default on a contract, this is an appropriate situation for the use of a liquidated damages clause. When the two parties recognize and agree on this difficulty in advance, they should negotiate to establish a formula for liquidated damages.

Liquidated damages should not be used as a penalty; not only is this objectionable to the vendor, it has been found objectionable by many courts. A financially sound and responsible company should be willing to reimburse a purchaser for any proven damages resulting from negligence of the company. If such damages are not covered voluntarily, litigation in court is normally a straightforward procedure for recovering such damages.

The vendor does find objectionable any agreement to pay liquidated damages as a penalty when that penalty has no relationship to the loss suffered, and when damages, if any, can be easily assessed. If the loss can be quantified, the recovery should equate to the loss. If the loss cannot be estimated, an appropriate liquidated damages settlement should be negotiated.

The problem in most cases is that the liquidated damages provisions are not negotiated, but are imposed on the vendor under a "take it or don't bid" situation. A satisfactory settlement cannot be prescribed by the buyer without giving the contractor an opportunity to negotiate the amount of settlement, yet this is a common situation.

Enhancements

Another sticky area is that of enhancements. There will frequently be a need to modify or customize either hardware or software in order to suit the user's needs more precisely as the contract work proceeds. It is important that these anticipated modifications be defined to the greatest extent possible in the contract. Also, a means of later emendation of the contract to incorporate enhancements should be determined so that the user is not left in a helpless situation.

The library should be satisfied that the system offered to meet its needs is the best currently available, and that it can be enhanced by additional or improved modules, or even by radical change. However, it should be understood that the vendor cannot guarantee unlimited compatibility with unknown future developments.

Expansion of the contract's scope should not be handled through informal verbal agreements. New features should be incorporated as an amendment or change order to the contract and provision made for an equitable adjustment to the purchase price.

What tends to happen is that the written descriptions, if any, are very sketchy. This may lead to a misunderstanding between the buyer and the contractor about the scope of modifications needed. The most frequent problem with enhancements concerns new features that have not previously been tested (or perhaps even developed). As these modifications are implemented and observed, the buyer may realize that there has been a misunderstanding and that his needs will not be fully met. This type of situation arises frequently on large contracts. It is a situation in which good faith — give and take — between both parties is essential. A more dangerous situation is that in which the buyer continues to expand his view of the functions that ought to be performed by the system as the system is in the process of being implemented.

Fitness for Purpose

Most contractors are frightened by contract language calling for the contractor to warrant fitness for purpose. There are basic problems with this approach and the clause should not be needed if the characteristics of the system to be provided have been carefully specified. The usual problem with fitness for purpose clauses occurs when the purpose is only hazily defined and most of the definition is in the mind of the buyer. This can lead to a situation in which the buyer demands a seemingly endless chain of modifications and adjustments beyond that contemplated by the contractor. To avoid this, a comprehensive description of the system should be incorporated and embodied as part of the contract. This will greatly assist in another area: acceptance.

Acceptance

Reaching an agreement that the work outlined by the contract has been completed will be facilitated by incorporating in the contract a fully detailed description of the functional performance of the system being supplied. Totally unworkable (in the vendor's eyes) will be acceptance by an individual based on his impressions rather than on system performance as compared with the stated specifications. The vendor will also almost certainly demand that the contract give the parties a means for getting a binding ruling in case of dispute, either through arbitration or litigation.

INSURANCE AGAINST DISASTER

There are many provisions that should be incorporated in a contract for the protection of each party. The best way of insuring against disaster has nothing to do with the contract. It is simply to find a good vendor. However, let me concentrate on what can be done in the contract.

Contract provisions should be made in advance so that if everything does not go according to the expectations of both parties, they have a mutually acceptable means for resolving whatever problems may arise. In addition to the terms of the contract, one must also consider prevailing laws. For example, the UCC contains an extensive body of law pertaining to contracts. In general, if a situation is covered by the law, nothing will be gained by making specific references to these provisions in a contract — unless the parties agree that the general provisions of the UCC should be modified, either expanding or limiting the remedies available under the UCC or the law.

There are many ways that difficulties may be encountered and as many as possible of these should be considered and addressed by the contract. For example:

Telephone services — It is frequently agreed that the purchaser will be responsible for scheduling the installation of needed telephone services, e.g., modems, dedicated lines, etc. If this work is not completed on schedule, it will delay the contractor.

Site preparation — Provision of clear operating space, electrical utilities and air conditioning is also often the scheduling responsibility of the purchaser.

Supplies — Magnetic tapes, disk packs, computer output paper, etc. will be needed for operation of the computer system. These materials might not be included as part of the system purchased.

File building — It is usually the responsibility of the purchaser to create the files of items and patrons necessary to operate a circulation system, for example. Depending on the circumstances, this may sometimes precede the planned installation of the circulation system.

Publicity — Usually, the library will wish to do some public relations work to explain the changes that will result from the purchase of a computer system and to acquaint the public with the justification for this purchase.

Training — Before a computer system can be put into operation, the operators must be trained. While this is normally the responsibility of the vendor, the library must make the staff available for training.

The above list of items will be sufficient to demonstrate that the purchaser has many responsibilities, as does the vendor. If the buyer does not fulfill these responsibilities, installation of the computer system may be delayed, or its swift implementation may be hampered. A good contract should protect the contractor against such purchaser-related performance problems.

The contract should also cover the expected payment schedule after satisfactory delivery and/or acceptance of the system. If the library accepts the system rather than rejects it but withholds payment because a few warranty items need to be corrected, the library is in breach of the contract — and at that point the vendor may not have to do any warranty work. Cooperation between the parties will help to avoid this sort of difficulty. It must be realized that the vendor has a major investment in a system of the type discussed here. Delay by the library in providing an operating environment for the system, or delay in paying for the system, can cause the vendor a financial loss against which he must protect himself.

Some problems may arise which are created by neither the library nor the vendor, e.g., fire, flood, strike or lockout, earthquake, war, transportation problems, etc. It is usual for both parties to agree that such problems may arise and that if they do, in essence, the contract goes into a holding pattern until the plague, pestilence or famine is removed.

In addition to the list of problems possibly created by the buyer or that might be considered as acts of God, there is probably an even longer list of problems that might be contributed by a vendor. The software (or programming bailiwick) usually causes most of the problems. I will not go into the problems a vendor may create here, because I was asked to make my presentation from the vendor's viewpoint.

WHAT TO DO IN CASE OF DISASTER

What can be done when, despite all the best planning, disaster strikes? Obviously, the first step to be taken in case of unsatisfactory performance by a vendor is to discuss the situation with the vendor. The vendor should be able to explain adequately the problems encountered, and to itemize the cures to be administered and the timetable to be followed.

If all does not go well, an aggressive and legalistic approach to the problem should not be taken immediately. Filing suit against the contractor without giving him an opportunity to propose a remedy causes many problems. First, it will create a needless expense for both vendor and purchaser. Energies of both parties will be directed at preparing legal defense rather than at finding a satisfactory solution. Furthermore, to a considerable extent, the hands of the vendor become tied when a contract goes into litigation. This only makes it more difficult to achieve a satisfactory resolution.

If the vendor does not meet the first timetable as stated in the contract, he obviously begins to lose credibility. Most vendors will move heaven and earth at this point in an attempt to make good. They realize that each satisfied customer provides a referral that aids their sales effort. A dissatisfied customer can act as a wet blanket on even the most aggressive sales campaign. For these reasons, a customer rarely needs to go beyond the vendor to obtain satisfaction. However, if the vendor is technically, morally or financially incompetent, then other recourse may be necessary. For example, if it becomes clear that the vendor is technically incapable of providing what he has contracted for, there may be several options; this depends on the contract documents. The termination provisions desired should be included in the contract. In the case of nonperformance, legal counsel should be obtained, but an aggressive stance should not be taken too hastily.

It may become clear at some point that a vendor just does not intend to meet a contract's provisions. Conceivably this could happen if the vendor did not wish to continue in the business because he could not make money at it. Steps in this case would be similar to those in the case of a technically incompetent contractor.

In the case of a financially failing contractor, options may be more limited. One should also be cautious that equipment provided by a financially shaky vendor has a clear title to it. Horror of horrors, the contractor might declare bankruptcy and leave the purchaser equipment that had liens against it placed by the company supplying the vendor with hardware. Worse yet, if a vendor has been paid and subsequently declares bankruptcy, the purchaser's equipment might be claimed by a lien-holder through a perfected security interest. In general, if reasonable prudence was exercised in selecting the vendor and negotiating the contract, all that will be required to get remedy is to confront the vendor with his shortcomings. (Of course, there will be situations where a company is unresponsive and the only way to get their attention is to file suit.)

CONCLUSION

It is possible for vendors and libraries to do business with each other successfully. It happens every day. A well-conceived, well-written contract will help the two contracting parties stick to their initial understanding. If the two parties are tenacious, reasonable and work well together, the contract will probably never be referred to once it is drawn. This does not mean that it has had no value; just as with auto insurance policies, one must take precautions for all eventualities.

It is also quite likely that the intellectual work involved in drafting the contract will be of major significance. It is quite common to find that only when one attempts to set an understanding down on paper does it become clear that there is no understanding.

As I have stressed, a vendor hopes that negotiations can be approached in an open, good-faith, above-board manner between two cooperating parties. There seems to be a growing attitude on the part of both federal and state government agencies to approach negotiating with a hostile and antagonistic attitude of mistrust, which causes vendors concern. There are some serious consequences resulting from such attitudes, including increased costs to the buyer. If the present trend continues, it may be impossible for government agencies to find vendors willing to submit to the harassment of doing business with those agencies. Even worse, these attitudes can lead to decay of the free-enterprise system and the ruin of those companies which are presently heavily involved in supplying government-funded organizations.

I would like to summarize with a simple, easily remembered message. A library and a vendor have a high probability of successfully negotiating a contract for the supply of goods or services. Were it not so, libraries would be empty. One might say, "Where there's two wills, there's a way."

ADDITIONAL REFERENCES

Brownrigg, Edwin B., and Bruer, J. Michael. "Automated Turn-Key Systems in the Library: Prospects and Perils," *Library Trends* 24:727-36, April 1976.

"Differing Site (Changed) Conditions," *The Government Contractor; Briefing Papers* 71-5, Oct. 1971.

Freed, Roy N. "Contracting for Computers and Electronic Data Processing Support Services," *The EDP Seminar Series,* Computerworld.

Kaskell, Ralph L., Jr. "Representing the Contractor in Dealing with the Architect, Owner and Sub-Contractors," *The Forum* 7:215-24, July 1972.

Latham, Peter S. "Multi-year Procurement," *The Government Contractor; Briefing Papers* 73-2, April 1973.

"Principles of Equitable Adjustment," *The Government Contractor; Briefing Papers* 71-2, April 1971.

Scaletta, Phillip J., Jr., and Walsh, Joseph L. "Syntax — Legal Analysis of Standard Commercial Computer Purchase and Lease Contracts." In *Understanding Computer Contracts, 1974.* Data Processing Management Association, 1975.

Shedd, Joel P. "Unconscionability in Contracts," *The Government Contractor; Briefing Papers* 75-3, June 1975.

Shnitzer, Paul A. "Competitive Negotiation," *The Government Contractor; Briefing Papers* 75-4, Aug. 1975.

_____. "Responsibility of Bidders," *The Government Contractor; Briefing Papers* 72-4, Aug. 1972.

Spector, Hon. Louis. "A Judge Looks at Large and Small Claims," *National Contract Management Association,* Nov.-Dec. 1976.

Pettit, Walter F. "Material Shortages and Spiraling Costs," *The Government Contractor; Briefing Papers* 74-4, Aug. 1974.

"Unconventional Methods of Procurement, Innovations in Government Buying Techniques," *The Government Contractor; Briefing Papers* 69-4, Aug. 1969.

JAMES F. COREY
Systems Librarian
University of Illinois
Urbana-Champaign, Illinois

Negotiating Computer Services within an Organization

THE OTHER PAPERS PRESENTED at this conference deal with negotiations between libraries and outside organizations, where the end product of negotiation is a written contract of some sort. This paper, by contrast, attempts to describe the possibilities for negotiation when the library uses the computer services of its parent organization.

Libraries have frequently had difficult relationships with their organizations' computer centers. For example, in 1962 the University of California at San Diego (UCSD) Library developed and commenced operating one of the country's first serial control systems.[1] The system was gradually improved and was running steadily when, in 1967, the Control Data Corporation computer at the university computer center was replaced with an incompatible one made by RCA. The library, in a frantic effort, reprogrammed its serials control system in time to have it running on the RCA computer. Just two years later, in 1969, the UCSD computer center changed from the RCA machine to a Burroughs computer. The library was again forced to reprogram. According to one account from UCSD: "The situation concerning lack of stability and scheduling of computers . . . contributed significantly to development costs, operational costs through conversion requirements, and . . . generally slowed progress."[2]

Another example can be taken from the University of Illinois at Urbana-Champaign where, in July 1973, the director of the university

Office of Administrative Data Processing sent a letter to the director of the library on the subject of a computer circulation system, promising that the Office of Administrative Data Processing "will commit to a May 30, 1974, deadline for delivery of a system to the library staff."[3] The system was delivered in May 1976 — nearly two years late. Unforeseen circumstances outside the control of the Office of Administrative Data Processing were in part responsible for the delay at Illinois, and the UCSD computer center may have had compelling reasons to switch computers twice. But an important question remains: What can the library do to protect itself from poor and costly service from its organization's computer center?

A library negotiating for computer services within its own organization cannot have a "contract" for services in the legal sense. Legal contracts can only be established between separate organizations. The final resolution of a contract dispute is court action. If two units of the same organization were to enter into a "contract" with one another, and subsequently the terms of the contract were not met, the organization would be faced with the situation of going to court to sue itself. Thus, libraries which use their organization's computer centers must find a substitute for the legal contract. Many libraries have embarked on projects with very little prior understanding of how the work was to be done and a vague feeling that problems would be solved as the work progressed. Some of these projects probably went smoothly. In others, issues may have been settled reasonably and amicably as they arose, with no detriment to the library. In other cases, however, serious problems based on misunderstanding have left both the library and computer center frustrated and angry. In the absence of a clearly written prior agreement, small projects are more likely to be completed than large ones, simply because there are fewer details which are potential sources for misunderstanding. The larger or more complex the project, the more important a clear understanding becomes.

Since a contract cannot be written between the library and computer center, what can be done? The answer is to draw up a written document that is like a contract in every way except in legal authority. Since the document is not a contract, it can be called an "agreement" or "joint memorandum of understanding." There are two reasons why a written agreement drawn up in advance of a project is valuable. First, the agreement will clarify what is needed for successful development and continuing support of a system. Better planning, especially development planning, will result and implementation schedules will be projected with more accuracy. Secondly, when problems arise, the agreement document can be used as persuasive leverage to obtain compliance from the other side.

Organizations which maintain a computer center as an internal unit of the organization may have one of two kinds of policies with respect to the degree of centralization of data processing resources. Some organizations permit their departments to employ analysts and programmers, but the computer equipment is centralized and shared by all the departments. In this case, the library will need only to negotiate for the use of the computer. Other organizations have a centralized pool of analysts and programmers as well as a centralized computer facility. Analysts and programmers are assigned by the computer center to departments on the basis of department needs, overall organizational priorities and, in some cases, departmental ability to pay for the services. In this latter case, the library must negotiate the services of analysts and programmers in addition to computer usage.

To cover all the detailed points that could go into a comprehensive agreement would require a document several times longer than this paper, but the general areas that should be covered by an agreement can be outlined and some commentary can be provided on the importance of each area. A suggested outline of major areas for negotiation is given in Table 1. Points on the outline will vary in importance depending on the nature of the application and whether the system is batch or on-line. Many points are interrelated. To reinforce the importance of reaching prior agreement, several examples taken from actual situations will be described to illustrate what can happen when issues are not agreed upon. In many of the examples, the library is not identified in order to avoid embarrassment to institutions with which the author has been associated.

Agreement for Machine Services

The hardware required to support the library is one of the first points to negotiate. The amount of main memory needed for the library's application should be discussed. While it is true that computers are becoming sophisticated to the point that main memory assigned to a program can be dynamically adjusted depending on the immediate demands placed on the computer, the library should nonetheless attempt to determine whether there are any restrictions on the amount of main memory that will be available.

Secondary memory, i.e., disks and tapes, can be a potential negotiating problem. Since library files are large, the library must negotiate forcefully, especially for disk space; otherwise the library may have to make serious compromises. One academic library was forced to use truncated titles in its circulation system and ended up with such titles as *A Priest for Ever: A Stud* (short for *A Study of Typology and Eschatology in Hebrews*) and *The People of Ancient Ass* (for *Assyria*). College students chuckle when they get overdue notices for such titles; the reaction of public library users might be less favorable.

TABLE 1. Major Areas for Negotiation

Agreements for machine services
1. hardware
   a. main and secondary memory
   b. communications lines
   c. terminals and other I/O devices
   d. character set
   e. stand-alone equipment
   f. maintenance
2. computer availability
   a. hours of service
   b. tolerable down time
3. operating system support
4. priority
   a. job scheduling
   b. response time
5. production
   a. schedule
   b. logistics (delivery of input and output)
   c. forms and supplies
6. price
7. growth
8. long-term hardware and software continuity

Agreement for personnel services
1. method for assignment of analysts and programmers
   a. delivery of finished product at specified time
   b. time and materials per project
2. change control
3. documentation
4. acceptance testing
5. program maintenance
6. program extensions

Communications lines must be specified as to type (dial-up, leased point to point, leased multipoint), speed and location of termination points. Lines must be compatible with terminals, so they should be specified at the same time. The number of hard copy terminals and the number of CRTs, along with the features to go on each, must be decided. Some terminals in key locations may require extra features, such as a tape cassette attachment to use when the computer is down. If the library needs other input/output devices such as optical scanners, the computer center must agree to support them. In some cases, the library may want the capability to add an attachment to their terminals in the future. The attachment may not work on terminals currently supported by the computer center. This could require the computer center to support a new type of terminal which otherwise would not have been selected.

The character set to be used should be planned carefully, because it may not be necessary to require the same character set on all input/output devices. Some libraries are satisfied with terminals with only upper- and lowercase and a few special characters to enter cataloging data. Foreign characters and diacritics are handled by the use of an escape character preceding one of the regular characters. However, when the cataloging data are printed on 3x5 cards, the full ALA character set is required and is mounted on the computer line printer. Other libraries want the full ALA character set on their cataloging terminals but will accept just upper- and lowercase on terminals used for searching or serials check-in.

When all of the hardware that is attached directly or remotely to the computer has been specified, the library should not overlook hardware that is separate from the computer. Optical character readers, Hollerith punch machines, bar-coded label printers, and computer output microfilm machines are just some examples of equipment that may be needed but are not attached to the central computer equipment itself.

The hardware "maintenance" specified in Table 1 refers in this instance to maintenance of computer equipment installed in the library. While the computer center obviously has responsibility to maintain equipment on its own premises, it cannot be assumed that the computer center accepts responsibility for computer equipment at the library. Now that on-line systems are becoming more prevalent, the most common pieces of equipment in libraries are terminals and modems. Libraries may also have keypunches, terminal controllers, concentrators, multiplexors and minicomputers. The equipment may be maintained by the computer center, the original manufacturer, or a third party. The University of Illinois Library has some terminals maintained by IBM, other terminals maintained by General Electric, others by the campus computer center, and still others by an independent maintenance firm located 120 miles away in Indianapolis. Some of the modems are maintained by Illinois Bell, and the rest are repaired on campus.

The requirements of the library for computer availability are quite important for on-line systems. One library discovered in the midst of developing a circulation system that its computer center was reluctant to run the system during all of the hours that the library was open. To meet library hours, the computer center would have to renegotiate its contract with the union governing computer operators, and would have to reschedule preventive maintenance and system test time. The computer center proposed that the library record circulation manually during certain hours and enter the transactions later when the computer was available. After moments of serious doubt, the library was able to convince the computer center to make the computer available during all open hours.

Down time can also be negotiated to some extent. Not all down time results from unanticipated hardware or software failure. Computers are often taken down deliberately to do system tests, switch equipment into or out of service, or perform maintenance. The library, by informing the computer center in advance of its peak periods and being willing to do without the computer during quiet periods, stands a good chance of getting a favorable agreement from the computer center for scheduled down time.

Operating system support is not normally a concern to the library. The library states its requirements in terms of functions to be performed and operational considerations such as hours of service. Occasionally, however, the operating system can be an issue. Most frequently it is an issue when a library tries to obtain programs written elsewhere. Programs written for one library may have been written to be used with a version of an operating system not in use at the other library's computer center, even though the two computer centers have computers of identical make and model. To cite two technical examples, programs written for IBM's OS won't run on IBM's DOS and programs written for VSAM won't run with ISAM. Negotiation will determine whether the operating system will be changed, the programs rewritten, or the hope of transferring the programs abandoned.

Anyone who had experience with OCLC in 1974 knows that response time is an important point that should be negotiated by the library. Response time is determined by so many complex interrelated factors that it is extremely difficult to predict in advance, even with complete knowledge of the design of the application. If response time is slow, the problem can be anywhere, e.g., file structure, indexes on a slow disk, communications line too slow, or insufficient main memory. The correction may require changes that the computer center is reluctant to make. Prior agreement on a reasonable response time is essential if a reluctant computer center is to be persuaded to make the necessary improvements.

The term "production" in Table 1 refers to the day-to-day running of a system once it becomes operational. Details concerning daily operation are frequently left until a system is near the end of the development stage. Scheduling is one such detail commonly ignored. Analysts and programmers will, of course, have an initial rough idea of the frequency of use of each program, e.g., monthly, weekly, daily, on demand, or at fiscal year end. Late attention to the specifics of program scheduling can, however, bring some unpleasant surprises. One library has a monthly accounting report that should be produced at the end of the month. It was discovered that, because the computer center already had a full schedule of month-end jobs, the library's job must run on the twenty-sixth of the month, reflecting transactions through the twenty-fifth. This arrangement is tolerable, but does require a special adjustment run at the end of the fiscal year to include transactions for June 26-30 in the year's accounting. This adjustment run must wait until mid-July, because the computer center is also saturated with year-end jobs.

Logistics are also frequently ignored. The library has an obligation to generate input for scheduled programs on time — but who transports the data to the computer center? Does the library carry the data to the computer center? Does the computer center come after it? Similar questions must be answered for output. One library found itself in the situation where the previous day's purchase orders were delivered each morning to the library by the computer center's courier service, while the previous day's overdue notices were not. The circulation system was developed two years after the book-order system. When the circulation system became operational, the courier service was declared to be fully loaded. After several months of negotiation, it was finally decided that the 6'2", 210-pound courier who delivered to the library could carry the extra two pounds of overdue notices — provided that he could leave them at the acquisitions department. The circulation department is delighted to send a 95-pound weakling down the hall each morning to get the overdue notices from the acquisitions department, presumably saving the weary courier from complete exhaustion. Another library in the Pacific Northwest lost their delivery battle. During the rainy winter season the library prints purchase orders only once a week because of the nuisance of trudging through the rain to the computer center to pick them up.

In the areas of price, growth, and hardware and software continuity, the library is essentially negotiating for the future. There have been many instances where libraries have been attracted to computer centers by offers of either free or unbelievably low prices. The offers were made when the computer centers had excess capacity. Invariably, computer usage continued to increase, excess capacity vanished, and the library was told to pay the standard rate, which amounted to an enormous increase.

The library should also attempt to elicit a commitment for future growth. This is especially important when the computer center has purchased its computer. One large university library developed a circulation system to be installed initially in its heavily used undergraduate library. After a year of operation, the library wanted to extend computerized circulation to all of its branches. It found to its dismay that, during the one year of operation, other university departments had developed numerous applications. The computer, a purchased machine, was saturated. The university could not afford just then to buy another computer; consequently, the library could not expand its circulation system.

Long-term hardware and software continuity is one of the most difficult points to negotiate. Computer center directors like to upgrade or improve their facilities. The impact on the user is often given little attention, especially in organizations where programming is not centralized within the computer center. Where programming is centralized, the computer center will have the responsibility to modify programs to run on new equipment. The library need not negotiate long-term continuity. However, libraries which do their own programming should seriously negotiate continuity. The experience of the University of California at San Diego should be enough to prove the point.

The library must not only be thorough in negotiating each of the above points individually, it must also cover interrelationships between points. For example, jobs usually can be assigned more main memory at a cheaper price at night than during the day. Terminals must be compatible with communications lines, and both must be supported by the teleprocessing software that is supplied with the operating system. While that much surely seems obvious, one library forgot to relate terminals, lines and teleprocessing software to job scheduling. The library bought terminals to be used for a technical services data collection application. Library staff keyed transactions into the terminals' local memory during the day. At the end of each day, the data stored in the terminals were to be sent down a phone line to a large computer. The terminals were installed, the proper phone line was installed, and the necessary teleprocessing software was tested and found to work beautifully. Then the problem was discovered — scheduling. The teleprocessing software used to read the library's terminals was incompatible with another teleprocessing system which was always scheduled to run until 8:00 p.m. The library's teleprocessing program couldn't be run until afterward. The process of reading the terminals' memory is normally automatic, but human assistance is required whenever anything goes wrong. The library had assumed that the terminals would be read near the close of each day, around 4:30-5:00 p.m., when someone would be available to monitor the operation. Instead, the staff now goes home knowing that one of them will be called to return to the library if a problem develops. On the average, the reading process is reliable, failing only about once a month. But staff members have been called out of bed at midnight to return to the library to push buttons on a malfunctioning terminal while diagnostic tests were performed from the computer center.

Agreement for Personnel Services

Libraries dependent upon centralized analysts and programmers must negotiate these services as well as machine services. The most important point to be decided is the basic arrangement by which development personnel are assigned to the project. There are two models. In the first model, called the finished product model, the computer center promises to deliver a specified product on a certain date. The number and kind of personnel assigned can vary from week to week or day to day. The library is not concerned about the number of personnel assigned, and in fact, may not even know what the staffing level is. The computer center may assign only one or possibly two people to communicate with the library, while an unknown number of people work on the project "behind the scenes." In the other model, called the time and materials model, no fixed dates are promised. Rather, the library is promised a level of effort, usually expressed in terms of the number of FTE staff to be assigned for the duration of the project. For example, a project may be assigned two programmers who work full-time until the project is finished. No deadline is set, but a project completion date is usually estimated to give computer center management an idea of when their personnel will be available for other projects, and to give the library an idea of when they will need to be ready for the new system.

The first model sounds more advantageous to the library, but in actuality it is not. The first model is really the second model in disguise. When the computer center works according to the first model, their personnel meet with the library several times to become acquainted with the proposed project. They return to their offices and make an estimate of the magnitude of the project, usually expressed in man-months. Next, they decide what personnel resources would be available to work on the project and for how long, and finally they calculate a completion date. Unfortunately, calculated completion dates, which are nothing more than estimates, are promised as firmly committed dates. Ninety-nine percent of the time, the dates will slip. The commitment is not firm in the sense that if the development schedule slips, the computer center will add more people to the project to get it back on schedule. Computer centers generally do not have enough personnel to move around in this manner. The University of Illinois example mentioned at the beginning is probably an unusually bad case, but any library which makes plans for personnel, equipment or building modifications based on a "firm" date may incur extra expense or inconvenience when the date slips.

It is far more practical to get a commitment for a fixed number of personnel for the extent of the project. Completion dates are regarded as they should be — as estimates and nothing more. No one is deluded and, for reasons described below, the library is in a much better position to make sensible decisions as the work proceeds.

Of all the areas listed in Table 1, one of the most important to the computer center is an agreement on change control. Change control refers to a set of rules (admonitions, really) which should guide the library when it seeks to make changes to the system during the development phase. The first rule indicates that the functions to be performed by the computer be specified correctly in the first place, so that no changes will be needed. The second rule is to get it 99 percent correct the first time so changes will be minor. The third rule is to do without overlooked functions until a later phase, when a whole set of improvements can be made at once. The fourth rule states that since the first three rules won't be followed, make change requests known as soon as the need is discovered and be prepared to accept compromise. Some changes can be made easily with a minimum of delay. More commonly, changes cause substantial delay and increase development costs. The library should be willing to agree to a clause on change control which adopts a philosophy that it is better to get a limited system running and gain practical experience than to request changes which have minor benefits. Projects always encounter a genuine need for some changes during development. The purpose of a change control clause in the agreement is more for psychological impact than procedural structure. The library needs to be warned in advance to be thorough at the outset and to restrict its demands during development to the very essential changes.

Documentation is of several types, two of which can be at issue. Types of documentation include functional specifications, system specifications, program documentation, production documentation and user manuals. The computer center is obviously responsible for system specifications, program documentation and production documentation. But functional specifications and user manuals can be the responsibility of either the library or the computer center, and this should be determined by agreement. Since a project cannot begin without functional specifications, agreement on responsibility is negotiated early. Nevertheless, at least one library forgot to discuss the user manual. The library assumed the computer center would write it; the computer center assumed the opposite. A lot of finger-pointing and unnecessary irritation resulted when the misunderstanding was discovered near the end of development. Implementation of the system was delayed six weeks while the library wrote a user manual.

Acceptance testing by libraries is frequently done superficially. The programmer tells the library a program is working. If it is a batch program, the programmer brings the library some demonstration output. The library looks at the program's reports to verify the presence of required data fields and check for bad data. To test an on-line program, a librarian will sit down at a terminal and enter data — both valid and invalid. If a program identifies invalid data while taking action with valid data, it is "accepted." None of these cursory tests constitutes a thorough acceptance test, because the data samples are too small. One can only say that a program works for the combinations of data with which it has been supplied. Acceptance testing should be performed by a team of experts within the computer center who are not part of the development team. A separate team would have necessary expertise but would avoid the conflict-of-interest situation which occurs when a programmer judges the acceptability of his or her own work. Most computer centers do not use such teams. The programmer's test, occasionally supplemented by library tests, are the usual acceptance tests. Libraries will probably never be able to negotiate thorough acceptance testing. But the library and computer center can and should still make an agreement on a sign-off procedure for the cursory tests. Thereafter, the library should realize that the first six months of operation of a new system will be the real acceptance test.

Program maintenance and program extensions are two areas in which the computer center has much more experience than the library. The computer center may have a policy or procedures manual that documents procedures to be followed. The manual, with modifications if necessary, can serve as the agreement for these areas. Program maintenance here refers to the correction of programming errors discovered after the system becomes operational. Corrections need a high priority. The computer center should agree to fast correction of errors and should be prepared to assign someone immediately to the problem, even if it requires taking a person temporarily from a development project.

Program extensions are design changes made to a system after it is operational. If a system was designed to be fairly complete at the beginning, changes will not be major — but this is usually not the case. The library should have a commitment from the computer center to incorporate extensions over a period of time. Because it is more effective from a programming point of view to make several changes at one time rather than one change at a time, the most pragmatic approach is for the library to accumulate ideas for improvements and to assign a priority to each. An agreement between library and computer center on program extensions entails an obligation on both sides. The library is obligated to batch requests instead of asking for one change at a time, one after the other. The computer center is obligated, after a period of time, to program the top several features which will most improve the system. One set of changes might be programmed, for instance, at the end of six months of operation, and another set at the end of twelve months.

A variation on the time and materials model for assigning analysts and programmers is possible, and it has ramifications for all of the other areas of personnel negotiation. Rather than assigning a fixed number of personnel for the duration of a project, the computer center can be asked to assign a fixed number of personnel for an indefinite length of time. The library, of course, would have to justify the request on the basis of some coherent long-range plans for automation. But if the case can be made for a long-term commitment, the need to negotiate a myriad of other details diminishes considerably.

The commitment will be for a fixed number of people with certain skills. The computer center does not have to promise specific individuals, but the arrangement works best when individuals can be found within the computer center organization who are interested in library data processing and will stay on the assignment. The benefits of such an agreement to the library are considerable. First, the library can explain library operations to the data processors in more detail, because the knowledge will carry over to later projects. Librarians who have seen a succession of computer center personnel, quickly tire of repeatedly explaining basic operations. Secondly, there is no need to negotiate formally change control, documentation, acceptance testing, program maintenance or program extensions. The computer center people are available to help the library in areas where help is needed most. The library can set priorities with full knowledge that more time spent on documentation will mean less time available for acceptance testing, or that time spent on extending an old system means time away from building a new one. Thirdly, computer center personnel know they will have to follow up on their work. If they do a poor job of testing, they will soon be required to do program maintenance.

Limitations of Agreements

Without a contract in the legal sense, there is no legal recourse to the solution of problems, and *a forteriori,* there are no penalty clauses. Agreements are like treaties; they can and will be broken. When they are, the problems must be solved inside the organization.

There are two possible places to appeal within an organization. The first appeal is to the computer center and, within the center, to the direct source of the problem, i.e., the computer operator, the programmer, or the systems analyst. Failure to solve the problem at the operational level requires the library to move its appeal up the hierarchy to computer center management. In most cases the problem can be resolved somewhere between the operational level and the computer center director. If the dispute reaches the computer center director, the library director will undoubtedly be involved.

When the problem is not resolved within the computer center organization, the second appeal is to higher administration. One may have to go up the organizational ladder until an administrator is reached who has jurisdiction over both the library and the computer center. In some organizations, the administrator may be several ranks removed from the library and computer center. In universities, it is not uncommon for the computer center director to report directly or indirectly to a vice-chancellor for administrative affairs, while the library director reports directly or indirectly to a vice-chancellor for academic affairs. The first common administrator is, then, the chancellor, the chief presiding officer of the university.

The library may encounter a number of problems in its appeal to higher administration. In the first place, higher management may, in general, regard the computer center more favorably than the library. The computer center may be looked upon as a unit devoted to modernization and an aid to institutional cost reduction, while the library is seen as a traditional and ever-increasing drain on funds. If this is the case, the library appeals from a position of weakness. Secondly, the more the dispute is embedded in computer technology, the more predisposed higher management is toward the computer center. In theory, if not in fact, computer center personnel are the experts on technological matters and librarians are not. Thirdly, disputed issues are likely to be too detailed to generate serious attention from higher management. Can the library effectively protest to a chancellor that response time is seven seconds when the computer center promised it would be three seconds? The head librarian is apt to get a pat on the head and be told to worry about book budgets or building plans, but not petty details. In short, unless the library is in high standing with the upper administration, it has a better chance for enforcement at the level of the computer center, particularly when the agreement clearly identifies the computer center's obligations.

There are other limitations to agreements that are potentially as serious as breach of agreement. Problems can arise that are outside the scope of agreements negotiated by the most diligent libraries. It is erroneous to assume that all possible problems can be anticipated and incorporated into an agreement. Some issues will be overlooked, and hence will not be agreed upon in advance. Other problems can be anticipated, but for one reason or another, cannot be negotiated. In many institutions, several areas of machine services cannot be negotiated, because computer centers often provide a set of basic services for all customers and adopt a take-it-or-leave-it attitude. As long as these computer centers have enough business, they refuse to negotiate special services.

Higher administration may itself be the source of problems. Higher administration may cut the computer center budget, reducing the center's capacity to serve the library with machine resources or personnel resources or both. Higher administration may, alternatively, cut the library's budget, reducing the library's ability to pay for planned automation. At one library, a serials list which had been started three years earlier was terminated for this very reason. The higher administration may decide on a top-priority computerization project which preempts a library project, even though the commitment to the library by the computer center had been a firm one.

The library cannot negotiate a clause stating that no human error will occur. By far the most common source of errors and problems in well-tested computer systems are human mistakes committed in the course of routine production operations. Jobs are forgotten and not run. Jobs are run late. Jobs are run on time, but the output is delivered late or is delivered to the wrong location. Preprinted forms get out of alignment on the printer, and the operator doesn't notice. Data can be mishandled by personnel. On one occasion, a large amount of data was keypunched and given to a courier who temporarily left the boxes of punched cards on a computer center hallway floor while he went into an adjoining room to speak to some colleagues. At this computer facility, scrap cards, being too voluminous for wastebaskets, were left in hallways for custodians to take away. The inevitable happened. During the few minutes that the courier had left his cards, the custodian came by. The cards were found in a large outdoor trash bin, wet and damaged.

The wrong files can be set up for a program, which then runs perfectly except for the fact that it is using the wrong data. One year, at the end of May, a computer center scheduled a normal program run in order to post the library's May book purchases and receipts to its year-to-date master file. The April year-to-date file should have been submitted to the program as the latest master file. Somehow, a computer operator selected the March year-to-date file. When the May fund reports arrived at the library, bibliographers were surprised, but pleased, to find they had more money than they expected. Coincidentally, free balances were about the same as the previous month's. Being near the end of the fiscal year, and as good bibliographers should, they all began ordering heavily to encumber the remaining money.

Worst of all, data can be completely lost. A typical scenario goes as follows. Two jobs are to be run back to back. The first job copies a master file from disk to tape for later processing, and the second job erases the disk copy of the master file to free the disk space for other use. The operator must not run the second job if the first job does not complete successfully. The operator fails to catch an error message from the first job; job two is released, and a portion or all of the data are permanently lost. There are more complicated variations of the story, but the results are the same — human error can result in the loss of data.

Solution and Conclusion

The library can take a number of steps to minimize the difficulties that may arise when it uses the machine and personnel resources of its organization's computer center. First, the library should get as much prior agreement as possible before starting on a project. If the library is already well into one or more projects, it is still possible to negotiate points not covered or renegotiate points by means of amendments. The essential purpose of agreements is not to assign blame when disputes occur, but to avoid misunderstanding in the first place by providing the computer center with a clear and complete itemization of services needed and expected.

If personnel services are supplied by the computer center, a commitment of a fixed number of people for an indefinite period of time is superior to any other arrangement. This arrangement comes close to actually having the personnel on the library staff, and it allows more continuity, improved understanding of the library, stronger motivation to do quality work, better communication and more flexibility to handle urgent unforeseen tasks.

In the area of daily operations, the library should negotiate the best schedules possible, insist on adequate backup and recovery procedures, and have library staff members examine output promptly and carefully in order to identify problems early. One should be prepared to communicate production problems quickly with adequate informational details — the absence of which makes it extremely difficult for computer center staff to diagnose a problem. If programs are written by the computer center, a clause should be negotiated which says that once data are in machine-readable form, they are the responsibility of the computer center, so that lost data which cannot be recovered by programmed recovery routines will have to be reconverted by the computer center without cost to the library. Privately, the library should plan for the worst, be ready to complain loudly and, if so inclined, seek divine assistance.

Formation of a users' group can be another effective step. Chances are very good that other units using the computer center will have similar requirements for good service and will be experiencing similar problems. The formation of a computer center users' group to discuss common problems and to make recommendations to the computer center can result in improvements that are not possible to negotiate individually. The users' group should have official recognition from the upper administration of the organization, in the same way that libraries have official advisory committees.

The last step is to try to solidify the library's standing with upper management. This might be accomplished by playing golf with them, joining the same church or civic club — whatever works. Since appeals are not made in a court of law, there is no rule which prohibits the "adjudicator" from being partial to the library.

A negotiated agreement by itself will not eliminate all the problems associated with use of computer center services, even though it is clearly written and comprehensive. An agreement can't even guarantee the elimination of major problems, but it will reduce the number of problems. An agreement will improve relations with the computer center, smooth development and operation of computerized systems, and reduce staff time spent on problem solving. An agreement is not a panacea. It is, however, an important element in the library's successful use of its organization's computer center.

REFERENCES

1. Vdovin, George, et al. "Computer Processing of Serial Records," *Library Resources & Technical Services* 7:71-80, Winter 1963.

2. Bosseau, Don L. "The University of California at San Diego Serials System — Revisited," *Program* 4:9, Jan. 1970.

3. Grazzino, Tony (Acting Director, Administrative Data Processing, University of Illinois). Memorandum to Lucien W. White, University Librarian, July 3, 1973.

LOIS UPHAM
Bibliographic Coordinator for MINITEX
University of Minnesota
and
ALICE WILCOX
Director of MINITEX
University of Minnesota
Minneapolis, Minnesota

Negotiating for Data Base Sharing

PERHAPS WE CAN BEST begin by providing a description of MULS (Minnesota Union List of Serials) in order to give an idea of its structure and to explain the interest of other organizations in using the data base for their projects. We will then attempt to describe the four types of negotiations in which it has become involved, and conclude with a few observations.

Background Information

MULS is a listing of serial titles held in nearly every library in Minnesota and in many in North Dakota. The project was begun in the summer of 1971, when the participants of the statewide network, Minnesota Interlibrary Telecommunications Exchange (MINITEX), voted to use a portion of their resource-sharing appropriations to produce a serials list. At that early point in the network's development, it was obvious that physical access was dependent upon bibliographic access and that the existing serial bibliographic tools were not adequate. Considering that three-fourths of the MINITEX requests were for journal citations, this was a significant problem.

Since August 1971, two hardbound editions and several fiche editions from the computer printout have been produced. A third bound edition of nine or ten volumes is scheduled for the summer of 1977. All of the editions are completely cumulative; there have been no supplements.

Beginning with the 1973/74 biennium, MULS has been supported by public funds as part of the MINITEX/Minnesota Higher Education Coordinating Board budget; additional state and federal LSCA funds have come from the Office of Public Libraries and Interlibrary Cooperation for public library participation. This use of public funds plays a significant role in the decision to share the MULS data base.

The data base presently contains 84,622 parent records and 52,013 cross-references and added entries. All types of serial records are included: periodicals, newspapers, annuals, document serials, monographs in series — in short, anything which is meant to continue publication indefinitely. Unnumbered series are excluded if the holding library does not use series-added entries in their catalog.

A wide variety of libraries have holdings included in MULS; this fact is reflected in the broad spectrum of titles which have been entered. The MULS data base has in its significant holdings not only those titles found in typical academic collections, but also those found in public and special libraries, including medical, agricultural, legal and theological titles. State, local and foreign document titles have been contributed to a large extent by Minnesota state agency libraries and by the university; newspapers have come chiefly from historical societies and from university collections.

The bibliographic information contained in MULS, although not as complete as that found on many catalog cards, is a good deal more complete than that traditionally contained in a union list of serials. It was felt that the extra coding and verification would be justified by the improvement in bibliographic control. A rather lengthy verification procedure is followed for each item; this is explained in the introduction to each edition and, in addition, the CONSER file is now being used as a primary verification source.

The holdings portion of the data base is actually significantly larger than the bibliographic portion. This results from the numerous holdings statements (sometimes more than 100) attached to each bibliographic record. The holdings statements are considered to be under the control of and, in a sense, "owned by" each respective library. The bibliographic portion is controlled by MULS/MINITEX.

The following elements, if present for the title in question, may be contained in the MULS record:

1. *Bibliographic/fixed field:* record type, date of entry into data base, conference publication indicator, modified record indicator, language of publication, country of publication, beginning date of serial, ending date of serial, publication status designator, type of periodical indicator, government publication designator, catalog source code,

physical media designator, type of material code and nature of contents code.

2. *Bibliographic/variable length fields:* Library of Congress card number, ISSN, language (041), main entry — personal name, main entry — corporate name, main entry — conference/meeting, title, abbreviated journal title, edition, imprint, general note, contents note (brief), note on indexing/abstracting coverage, note on volumes/numbers, note on supplements, note on indexes, added entries and cross references. In addition, there is a "location of holdings" tag which provides internal control for retrieval of records for individual locations.

3. *Holdings portion:* NUC symbol for library, a locally assigned 3-letter mnemonic, a subdivision of the primary location, the actual holdings down to issue level if desired and always including date, call number and notes pertaining to that particular holding.

Careful editing and rigorous problem-solving are done throughout the entry process and all printouts are proofread. Upon initial entry into the data base, each library is given a printout of their data as entered for corrections, additions and deletions. At this point, the update procedures begin and each library is strongly urged to participate. Update information is processed continually and, in fact, there has not been one working day in the five and one-half year history of the project during which update information has not been processed.

Perhaps the most important point to be made about the data base is that from the very beginning the decision was made that the then-new MARC format for serials would basically be used for MULS. There are some local variations, mostly in the form of omissions of some fields, but other fields were actually augmented. Nevertheless, by using MARC tagging and subfielding, output tapes in MARC communications format can be produced. Since 1971 some changes and additions have been made to the original format which have brought it into closer alignment with MARC-Serials (MARC-S). As the staff moves to on-line control of the data base, it is expected that any remaining differences can effectively be eliminated.

Principle (CONSER)

Although several inquiries had been made, the first seriously considered request for non-Minnesota use of the MULS data was made by the Council on Library Resources (CLR), the administrative agency for the CONSER Project. Most libraries are aware of the project, especially since its coverage in the January 1977 issue of *American Libraries;* the need for such an undertaking was identified and the mechanism established. OCLC is currently housing the file on its system;

selected libraries are participating in the project on-line, and CLR is the CONSER manager.

At start-up time, however, it seemed most desirable to have a data base to begin with. MARC-S record service had not then been operational for long, and the file was still small. After some investigation, CLR approached MINITEX to ask that they consider contributing the MULS file to CONSER, since it appeared to be the largest existing data base which was basically in the MARC format and which contained rather complete bibliographic records.

Data base sharing was a new concept at that time and admittedly there were some problems. Looking back, most of them now seem of little consequence. First, there was confusion about who should negotiate for use of the data base. MULS is a program of the Minnesota Higher Education Coordinating Board (MHECB) which contracts with the university for its administrative services. There is a MINITEX Advisory Committee, and individual libraries contributed their records. The university held the copyright. After covering all the possibilities, the university library administration in conjunction with the MINITEX/MULS staff (with MHECB concurrence) became the negotiating agent.

The second problem was even more complex in that it concerned a matter of personal feeling. OCLC had earlier approached MULS directly to explore the possibility of procuring the data base for its system. After discussion, a proposed fee was established. OCLC never responded, however, and the inquiry came to naught. Now, as part of the CONSER arrangement, OCLC would be getting the data base. Nonetheless, the opportunity to participate in what promised to be a landmark project left little choice: it was decided that the data base would be given.

The final problem was that of real costs to MULS. It was quite obvious that for some time the in-house system would have to be maintained along with the on-line input to the CONSER records. The first priority was to continue supporting the MINITEX resource-sharing system through the MULS bibliographic access. CLR in an eminently reasonable manner compensated MULS for its CONSER updating activity by providing one terminal and subsidizing the maintenance and line charges on two terminals.

In the summer of 1975 a magnetic tape of the MULS file was delivered to CLR and the MULS staff continued to input new records and to augment their tape-loaded records.

It might be said that the CONSER agreement was one concluded for the sake of principle. The cooperative creation, augmentation and authentication of a file of MARC-S records is one that any library-oriented person would support. MULS had been produced using public funds and it was only fitting to contribute it to a national program. The CONSER negotiations were mostly verbal and the final agreement was merely in the form of letters exchanged between the university library administration and CLR. Upon reflection, it is doubtful that anyone would disagree with this decision. Making a decision for the sake of a principle is a good idea.

Partnership (North Dakota and Wisconsin)

The second major use of the MULS file outside Minnesota was for the creation of a union list of serials for the state of North Dakota. Minnesota and North Dakota have a reciprocity agreement which allows students to attend schools in the neighboring state at in-state tuition rates and includes an understanding about sharing various resources. As a part of the agreement which covered sharing library resources and bibliographic services, a North Dakota Union List of Serials (NDULS) was created by adding North Dakota holdings and unique records to the MULS data base. As a precursor to the interstate agreement, North Dakota State University (part of the Tri-College University consortia) had already participated in MINITEX, and their holdings were included in MULS.

Critical to the agreement was a resource-sharing clause that included the development of a serials data base. All the serial literature is available for use by both states; thus, North Dakota data became an integral part of the MULS file. When the physical items are not accessible, however, a totally different approach must be taken.

In the North Dakota/Minnesota library contract, MHECB through its MINITEX network agreed to:

1. prepare a union list of North Dakota serials (NDULS) and deliver it in camera-ready copy to be published and distributed by the North Dakota State Library Commission at its own expense (the North Dakota records were then to be added to MULS);
2. maintain the NDULS data base during this and consequent agreements and (at mutually agreeable times and costs) supply updated camera-ready copy or microfiche;
3. provide at mutually agreeable times sublistings of titles within given specifications;
4. supply a copy of the NDULS on tape to the North Dakota State Library Commission (note that the bibliographic portion was to be controlled by MULS — the holdings by NDULS); and
5. enter into negotiations for computer programs to support a possible independent NDULS system. It was further agreed that NDULS would be completed and delivered to the North Dakota State Library Commission within thirteen months of the date of the contract.

The remainder of the agreement dealt with resource-sharing and finally affixed an amount to be paid to MHECB.

The MULS/North Dakota relationship was essentially a partnership because of the reciprocity agreement. This proved very workable and most satisfactory, for both sides were cooperating to produce a tool which would enhance their library service. The payment to Minnesota was based on the inequities of resources and services. This partnership agreement, like the one based on principle, seems to be sound and agreeable.

The Wisconsin Little Magazine Project (an agreement to input records for a large and significant collection of little magazines held at the University of Wisconsin-Madison) is basically the same as the agreement with North Dakota, for Minnesota also has a reciprocity agreement with Wisconsin. While the funding was different in that it came from an NEH grant, the circumstances were similar and those records became an integral part of the MULS data base.

Vendor (Montana)

The third type of negotiation to share the MULS data base has undoubtedly been the least satisfactory. This was the agreement to produce the Union List of Montana Serials (ULMS). Since Minnesota and Montana do not share resources, this became a service-bureau type of negotiation. Minnesota could efficiently produce a union list of serials for Montana by adding their holdings to the existing bibliographic records and creating new records with holdings for any unique items. There were also obvious advantages for Minnesota. It is very expensive to pay an adequate staff to maintain a union list of serials. MULS has been successful partly because it has been a continuous program with all participants regularly submitting update data. The Montana agreement could help to level the work flow and thus permit retention of some staff who otherwise could not be justified.

In many ways, however, minds were still in the past, and perhaps the Minnesota negotiators were not careful enough during the discussion period and with the written agreement. Minnesota wanted to share its information for the same reason that the CONSER Project was begun, i.e., to avoid continued replication of the same bibliographic records. The details varied, however; the agreement was to produce a product for a customer and no partnership was involved: MINITEX had become a vendor! A subtle change takes place when a customer puts money down for a product. The sense of sharing and cooperation is somehow lost and the buyer begins to think in terms of comparing vendors' bids and to expect a sales staff. MINITEX obviously had no sales staff and was not skilled in bid preparation or competition for jobs. Previously, responses had only been made to requests for the MULS data base in cooperative or partnership modes. While MINITEX reluctantly agreed to send a staff person to Montana to explain MULS and the procedures for handling Montana input, there was no forewarning of the competitive situation which developed. The two-part session included private presentations by Blackwell/North America and MULS with a final summary by both representatives. While Lois Upham was simply providing an explanation, the Blackwell representative was trying to make a sale.

In spite of a higher cost Montana chose MULS, probably for the following reasons: (1) MULS's proven success and ability, (2) its willingness to make extensive efforts in clarifying bibliographic entries before returning them to the contributing library, and (3) because any unique Montana records would become part of the CONSER file. The asking price was not attractive to many Montana libraries; in fact, it was bluntly questioned why MULS was asking "so much." The project was nevertheless less than financially satisfactory to MULS for several reasons:

1. The number of titles actually submitted exceeded by 50 percent the figures upon which the original estimate was based.
2. New lists continued to arrive after the proposed cutoff date — even though the cutoff had already been extended one month.
3. Many of the submissions were almost illegible and required a great deal of time to decipher.
4. Many entries were not submitted in AACR/LC form and thus required a greater degree of professional judgment to determine correct entry for search and input.
5. Not all the problems which were returned to the contributors for clarification were answered satisfactorily.

Moreover, due to the above factors, processing took much longer than was originally estimated. Not only did this mean more staff hours, but a new fiscal year and increased salaries created havoc with the budget.

The Montana union list agreement contained almost exactly the same provisions regarding creation of the serials list as did the one with North Dakota — except that the North Dakota agreement was part of a larger sharing arrangement. An agreement that was satisfactory between partners was not sufficient for a vendor/buyer relationship. Different relationships led to different expectations. Lacking specific numbers and dates and/or penalty statements, there was little recourse, so the data — extra, late, poor quality, etc. — were handled by a small staff which had not expected these problems. In addition, there was some confusion about verbal promises made during the meetings.

Thousands of hours of work went into the project, and Minnesota has learned a valuable lesson. Our experience suggests that future agreements such as this should be modified. First, all conversations, meetings and discussions should be carefully recorded in detailed minutes, on tape, or both. Secondly, the details of the agreement (the number of records to be submitted, the form in which they are to be submitted and submission deadlines) should be carefully set down. If changes occur, renegotiation should take place or a penalty clause of some sort could be written into the text. For example, this could take the form: "It is expected that 25,000 records will be submitted; however, if this number exceeds 26,000, the amount of $x will be assessed for each record over 26,000."

"Family" (MINITEX Participants)

The final type of negotiation is between MULS and an individual or group of MINITEX participants who want to receive subset listings of the entire data base. The capacity to produce such lists for any configuration of libraries has been available from the beginning of the project. It is a reasonable service and many lists have been produced, but there are some difficulties.

These lists are produced at cost and generally coincide with another production. The program required to estimate costs accurately is frequently more expensive than the actual run itself. Therefore, if a group insists on exact estimates and definite production schedules, the cost is obviously greater.

Observations

In retrospect, MINITEX/MULS has been involved in four types of data base negotiations: (1) negotiations based on principle, (2) negotiations as a partnership, (3) negotiations as a vendor, and (4) negotiations as a member of the "family." Each type has its individual characteristics, working environment and rewards that determine the relationship between the parties.

When libraries negotiate for services or products, it is critical that they understand their options and weigh all the possibilities carefully in order to make the best choice. While it is a cliché, most misunderstandings could have been avoided if the objectives, responsibilities and expectations had been clearly defined at the beginning.

As a subset of American society, the library community has two basic models. The capitalist, profit-making tradition is well established. We are all conditioned by vigorous salesmanship, slick marketing, keen competition, a full range of products and services, and the attitude of *caveat emptor*. We also have a long and noble tradition of cooperative efforts producing credible results, frequently with limited finances. This is the energy that helped to settle the West, man volunteer fire departments and reduce pain and suffering through organized charitable activity. The models are not mutually exclusive; they exist side by side.

The rapid development of cooperatives and networks which started in the early 1960s is evidence that librarians are increasingly looking at cooperative ways to share resources and services. Uncertain funding, constrained budgets, the information explosion and ever-increasing user demands exert pressure on the library community to look to the commercial sector or cooperative arrangements as a panacea. Both are expensive. Purchased expertise is expensive and a product may be inappropriate for the desired application. Cooperative decision-making and activity is time-consuming and requires patience. The products are sometimes fragmented and amateurish. Perhaps librarians are sometimes too quick to abdicate their independence when they have the ability to solve their own problems. They possess the professional expertise that is needed. It is not always necessary to relinquish everything to commercial enterprises. Perhaps a blend of the two could exploit the best qualities of each.

While MINITEX/MULS relies heavily on the commercial sector to assist in some of the computer and printing processes, we can positively attest that negotiations with other librarians are most rewarding when they involve sharing and cooperation. It is our professional tradition and appears to be mutually beneficial to all.

JANET EGELAND
Vice President
Bibliographic Retrieval Services, Inc.
Scotia, New York

Negotiating for On-Line Data Base Services: The Vendor's Viewpoint

THE SUCCESSFUL APPLICATION OF on-line technology to the storage and retrieval of information from large, machine-readable bibliographic data bases resulted in the availability in the late 1960s of an entirely new type of computerized information service to the library community. The possibility of interrogating large collections of references to the scientific and technical literature by remote on-line computer terminals promised both the reference librarian and the library patron welcome relief from the time-consuming task of manually searching through countless volumes of printed indexes and abstracts in order to satisfy their information needs.

Unfortunately, the initial dissemination of the new technology was slow. From the mid-1960s to 1970, on-line data base retrieval services were largely controlled by and limited to the nonprofit sector. Services were extended to libraries affiliated with government agencies such as DDC and NASA, where comprehensive on-line networks were evolving around specialized science and technology data bases. Health science libraries were eligible for access to the MEDLARS data base which was developed by the National Library of Medicine (NLM) and was available on-line from NLM and the State University of New York in Albany.

The wider-scale dissemination of these services began in the early 1970s with the emergence of commercial on-line data base vendors who acted as primary middlemen in the provision of service. Organizations such as System Development Corporation (SDC) and Lockheed Information Services began offering interactive searching on a profit-making basis from a wide variety of bibliographic data bases on a nationwide scale via common carrier telecommunication networks. This made it possible for a larger number of libraries in both profit and nonprofit sectors and in diverse geographic locations to take advantage of the new technology. Even with this improved mechanism of dissemination, the charges for the commercially available services were relatively high in comparison to those for the publicly sponsored services, and it was only the information centers of major industries and the larger academic research libraries which became heavily involved with on-line data base services in the early 1970s.

During 1975-76, a tremendous upsurge of interest in on-line data base services took place. Perhaps due more to peer pressure than in response to carefully studied needs, libraries of all sizes and types began to investigate the possibility of acquiring these new services. During this same period (May 1976), Bibliographic Retrieval Services, Inc. (BRS) entered the marketplace as the third major commercial vendor of on-line data base services. The marketplace then was composed of a large number of potential consumers who had highly variable and often ill-defined service needs and who were looking for cost-effective methods of leaping onto the on-line bandwagon. The entrance of BRS into this marketplace was significant because BRS offered on-line services at substantially reduced connect-hour prices, spurring an eventual industry-wide reduction in access fees in January 1977. More important, libraries were now faced with more alternatives for on-line data base service sources and they began to negotiate for the services best suited to their needs. Until that time, on-line services, their prices and access arrangements, had been fairly standard across the industry, leaving little or no room for the vital process of negotiation.

The remainder of this paper is devoted to some brief observations regarding the process of negotiation for on-line data base services in the current market environment. The readers should be aware that the observations and opinions expressed here are based on the recent experiences of one on-line vendor — BRS — and may not be representative of other vendors.

ARE ON-LINE DATA BASE SERVICES NEGOTIABLE?

If the vendor of an on-line data base service has offered a specific service at a specific price, it is probably pointless to attempt to negotiate a lower price. Among other things, legal restrictions prevent any customer from receiving service on terms more favorable than those afforded the federal government. On the other hand, negotiation can result in new services, new combinations of services and new rate structures. The innovations thus created would, of course, be made available to all customers on the same terms.

As a new vendor, BRS has gone through a series of negotiations with a variety of libraries since May 1976. The process of negotiation is a necessary part of the vendor/customer relationship with regard to securing on-line service for the following reasons:

1. Information retrieval services are precisely what the name implies — *services,* not products. Negotiation is a natural part of the vendor/ customer relationship in any service industry. Services can be individually tailored to meet the customer's special needs; in contrast, products are produced to satisfy a standard customer need. Buying an on-line data base service is not like buying a security system or a minicomputer system for the library.

2. The customer's need for information services is highly situation specific and thus variable. It is not possible to offer a standard service at a standard price that will satisfy all these variable needs. The term *negotiation* implies flexibility which is an extremely important factor in the vendor/customer relationship. Perhaps one of the reasons for the early success of the OCLC system could be the fact that libraries that wanted to participate in the new service were not forced to accept a predetermined cataloging standard, but were able to retain their own particular standard of cataloging.

3. Customers expect to have something to say when purchasing services. Although most car buyers acquiesce to standard purchasing arrangements, the same buyer would expect a great deal more flexibility and control upon hiring a chauffeur. Certainly, the librarian expects more flexibility when contracting with a subscription service than when merely purchasing journals outright from the publishers.

Negotiation is not only necessary but desirable from BRS's point of view because when it is successful, it results in a higher level of satisfaction with the service and an increased degree of trust between vendor and customer. An element of suspicion tends to exist among librarians about the role of the commercial information vendors. If negotiation can help to increase the trust between the vendors and the customers of these services, then it is definitely beneficial to both parties.

NEGOTIABLE AND NONNEGOTIABLE ASPECTS OF ON-LINE DATA BASE SERVICES

This subject is best dealt with by first delineating the major components of the service itself and then dealing with each one individually. The major cost components of the on-line data base services are:

1. connect-hour costs to access the vendor's computer;
2. communications costs to get from the customer location to the vendor's computer;
3. data base royalty costs assessed by data base producers;
4. off-line printing costs (optional); and
5. training and educational services costs.

Connect-Hour Charges

Prior to the entrance of BRS into the on-line data base services market, the connect-hour charges for access to the vendor computer were standard for all users, regardless of the amount of use made by the customer. Since there are, in any system of this type, scale economies related to the over-all volume of usage, BRS wanted to make the connect-hour prices negotiable, with rates determined on the basis of the number of hours of usage by each customer. By offering lower connect-hour rates for higher volumes of usage, we hoped to encourage the increased utilization of the on-line services in the library.

Thus, BRS began negotiating in April 1976 with a group of potential high-volume customers who wanted assurances of low connect-hour price in return for this volume commitment. We struck a "bargain," if you will, with this group which resulted in our first type of service arrangement, called the "high-volume fixed annual subscription." Specifically, this arrangement provided for up to seventy connect-hours of access per month for the fixed annual payment of $7500 ($8.90 per connect-hour). Clearly, this type of arrangement was tailored to the needs of a very special type of customer and was not applicable to the average potential service users.

In order to provide for price flexibility to other potential libraries of different types and sizes, BRS developed a "sliding scale" connect-hour pricing policy which would accomplish our general policy of lower prices for higher volumes. This scale is reproduced in Table 1. This sliding scale seemed to meet the needs of most libraries, and it removed the need to negotiate a connect-hour rate for each interested customer. We did find after the first several months of experience with this pricing scale that the smaller libraries were intimidated by even the five-hour per month level, and as a result we extended the bottom limit down to three hours per month (thirty-six hours per year) at the connect-hour rate of $30.00. This pricing policy has proven highly successful and has since been adopted by other vendors. Its success can be attributed to the customer's possession of some element of control over the price of the service.

Another major area of negotiation with regard to connect-hour prices involves the availability of discount rates for groups or consortia. BRS initiated a group discount policy which provided members of established

TABLE 1. BRS Connect-Hour Rate Scale

Volume of usage per month	Rate per connect-hour*
70 hours (fixed annual)	$ 8.90
40 hours (480 hour annual)	13.00
20 hours (240 hour annual)	16.00
10 hours (120 hour annual)	20.00
5 hours (60 hour annual)	25.00

* These rates do not include communication charges or any applicable data base royalty fees.

library networks or consortia with access at reduced connect-hour rates in return for the larger number of hours that could be purchased by a group in comparison to an individual library. To date, four major library networks are participating in this group service arrangement: Northeast Academic Science Information Center (NASIC), University of California Library System, Federal Library Committee, and Midwest Region Library Network (MIDLNET). In addition to reduced connect-hour rates available to group members, many of the networks also provide even more service flexibility for their members by centralizing the billing, providing additional training, etc.

Communication Costs

Access from the customer's location to the vendor's computer is generally via one of the two major national telecommunication networks, Telenet or Tymnet. These networks charge the vendor by the connect-hour for this service. In the case of Telenet, these fees are FCC-regulated and thus essentially nonnegotiable. BRS simply charges these direct costs back to each customer, adding $1.00 per hour to cover the equipment necessary to handle the Telenet connection at the BRS Computer Center.

Data Base Royalty Fees

There are several data base producers who require that on-line users pay a "royalty" fee for the use of their data base via any on-line information service. Rather than incorporating these royalty fees into the BRS connect-hour rate, we assess them separately and remit them directly to the data base producers. Current connect-hour royalties for data bases available on BRS are found in Table 2.

The connect-hour royalties are added to the BRS connect-hour rate which is determined by the total hourly level of usage. For example, if a customer subscribes on a 40-hour per month basis (480 annual hours),

TABLE 2. Data Base Royalty Charges

Data base	Rate per connect-hour
BIOSIS Previews	$15.00
CA Condensates	4.00
Dissertation Abstracts	50% of user's connect-hour rate
INFORM, Pollution ABS	30.00
INSPEC	15.00
NTIS	10% of user's connect-hour rate
Psychological Abstracts	20.00

then royalty rates for the use of any of the data bases in Table 2 will be added to the BRS connect-hour rate of $13.00. These royalty charges are not negotiable with BRS. In fact, in the case of the royalty fees, BRS is actually the customer and has no control over the charges assessed by the data base producer.

Off-Line Printing Costs

All on-line vendors have standard fees for off-line printing done at their computer center. These charges vary from vendor to vendor, however. Usually a set fee is charged per citation printed off-line. BRS, however, charges by the page for off-line printing — $0.10 for the MEDLARS data base and $0.15 per page for all other data bases. Although these rates are not negotiable, the fact that BRS charges by the page gives the user an element of flexibility and control over the off-line charges, since the actual cost per citation will depend on which data elements are printed. Table 3 shows the average number of citations that can be printed per page depending on the data base and the data elements requested.

Training Costs

Libraries vary in their need for training in the use of on-line services and should be able to negotiate with the vendor for an appropriate level of training. BRS has a standard policy with related charges for both system and data base training, but special arrangements are always possible with reference to the length of the training period required and the number of trainees involved. Standard arrangements are not always appropriate, and the overwhelming importance of adequate training to the eventual success or failure of the on-line service makes it essential that vendors provide as much flexibility as possible in the training arrangements.

Other Negotiable Aspects of the On-Line Service

Aside from the major cost components discussed above, there are other considerations equally important to the customer in the negotiation

TABLE 3. AVERAGE NUMBER OF CITATIONS PER PAGE
FOR SELECTED DATA ELEMENT CONFIGURATIONS

	Data element configurations			
Data base	*Default**	*AU,TI,SO*	*AU,TI,SO,DE†*	*All*
BIOSIS Previews	8.5	10.0	8.0	4.5
CAIN	7.5	10.5	10.0	3.5
CA Condensates	7.5	12.0	9.0	4.0
Dissertation ABS	8.5	13.0	7.5	6.5
ERIC	8.0	13.0	7.5	2.5
INFORM	11.5	13.0	—	2.5
INSPEC	8.0	12.0	10.0	2.0
MEDLARS	9.5	12.0	7.0	2.5
NTIS	7.5	13.0	7.5	1.5
Pollution ABS	10.0	13.0	7.5	4.0
Psychological ABS	10.0	12.0	9.0	2.5

* These are the predetermined default paragraph sets listed in the *BRS System Reference Manual,* Appendix VI.
† DE in this case represents descriptors — depending on the data base, there may either be a single DE element or both an MJ and an MN element.

for on-line services. Two of the most important are: (1) nature and length of service obligations, and (2) invoicing and payment procedures.

At BRS, these were found to be the areas where the customer required the most flexibility. Libraries, particularly government and academic libraries, vary greatly in their budgeting requirements, fiscal years, purchasing and payment procedures, etc. It is simply not feasible for a vendor to require standard service periods and payment schedules from libraries having financial requirements of their own. BRS will individualize here, even if it results in additional bookkeeping. Our customers may negotiate to pay monthly, quarterly, annually, or set up deposit accounts. Service periods may correspond to the customer's fiscal year, the calendar year, or any other period preferred by the library.

One of the most popular access arrangements for BRS users has been the subscription. This alternative was suggested by many of the libraries with which BRS negotiated. Since subscriptions are a standard method of purchasing other information resources in the library, it was suggested that this type of arrangement be extended to on-line services. As a result, BRS announced a new subscription access policy in January 1977. Subscriptions are generally paid from a definable and established budget, and many libraries have found that purchasing a subscription to an on-line service makes it easier to incorporate the cost of the service in the library budget. Currently, more than 70 percent of our customers are accessing BRS on an annual subscription basis.

One of the biggest stumbling blocks to the increased utilization of on-line data base services is the difficulty that libraries have in budgeting for or financing computerized reference service. It seems to be harder to find the support for these services than for the computerized applications in other areas of library service, such as cataloging, serials, acquisitions, etc. As a vendor of these services, BRS wants to help ease the budgeting problems by providing as many alternative arrangements as possible.

KEY ELEMENTS IN THE NEGOTIATION PROCESS

In summary, our experience indicates that negotiation is a vital and important process in the vendor/customer relationship regarding the selection of an on-line data base service. The key elements in this process are the flexibility to allow for situation specific needs and cross-situational consistency to ensure trust between vendor and customer that service arrangements are comparable when situations are the same.

CONTRIBUTORS

BRUCE BAJEMA has had experience as a county librarian in Marin County, California since 1968. He has written several articles on the computer's place in the public library, including: "Marin County Free Library Cost Effectiveness of a Dedicated Minicomputer for Acquisition and Circulation" and "Library Space Use for New Technology." Mr. Bajema served on the committee forming the CLASS (California Library Authority for Systems and Services) governing board and is now acting chairman of the CLASS data base task force.

RICHARD BOSS currently serves as University Librarian at Princeton University. Prior to July 1975, he served as Director of the Library at the University of Tennessee at Knoxville. Mr. Boss became familiar with negotiating for computer services while working as an acquisitions librarian where he was instrumental in approving plans for automated services.

RONALD BRADY has acted as Vice-President for Administration for the University of Illinois since July 1972. His previous positions include Vice-Chancellor for Administration at Syracuse University and Executive Assistant for the President at Ohio State University. As well as teaching as a professor of public administration in business and economics, Mr. Brady has served as guest lecturer and consultant for IBM and other computer management services and has written numerous articles and papers on the subject.

JAMES COREY is Systems Librarian at the University of Illinois at Urbana-Champaign. His experience in computer systems includes serving as data processing systems analyst for the University of California Library Systems Development program and as systems engineer for IBM. He has authored several publications on the subject.

JAMES DIVILBISS is Associate Professor, Graduate School of Library Science, University of Illinois at Urbana-Champaign since 1971. He is active in the fields of library automation and information retrieval and is a member of the Association for Computing Machinery.

CHARLES DYER has recently accepted a position as Law Librarian and Associate Professor of Law at the University of Missouri-Kansas City School of Law. Mr. Dyer has successfully combined his dual interests in law and computers in teaching the legal aspects of the computer industry and emphasizing student training in the use of the LEXIS data base. Currently, Mr. Dyer is involved in research into the legal aspects of considering information data bases as public utilities.

JANET EGELAND is currently Vice-President of BRS, Inc. of Scotia, New York. She has been involved in this computer service organization since its inception. Ms. Egeland is responsible for the planning and supervision of BRS educational programs and marketing and public relations activities. Prior to holding this position, Ms. Egeland was part of the Office of Computer Systems Development at SUNY where she was director of SUNY/Albany Biomed Communications Network. She has spoken several times at ALA, MLA and ASIS conventions over the past years and has written several articles for library journals.

GLYN EVANS has been Director of Library Services at SUNY Central Administration since 1972. Prior to this, he served as coordinator of Library Systems for Five Associated University Libraries at Syracuse University. Mr. Evans's considerable experience with library computer systems includes authoring of the final report of a grant project on collection development analyses based on OCLC archival tapes, and search training on the MEDLARS retrieval computer system for the London and southeast England area.

GRAHAM GURR is manager of 3M Company's Library Systems which markets "Tattle-Tape" book detection systems to prevent unauthorized book borrowing from libraries. Dr. Gurr earned his Ph.D. in physics at the University of Adelaide, South Australia (his home town) and did postdoctoral work at the University of Pittsburgh. He joined 3M in 1963 to do basic research in structural physics. He was named to his present post in 1973 and regards it as "a logical progression from pure physics, to applied science, to marketing and then to a business-oriented position."

LOIS UPHAM has long served as a professional serials librarian, but it was not until her current position as bibliographic coordinator for the MINITEX network that she became involved with computer data base systems. She is responsible for working with the Minnesota Union List of Serials and for training MINITEX library users that are part of OCLC. She has written several articles and spoken at conferences on the subjects of CONSER and MULS.

ALICE WILCOX, director of MINITEX, became involved in networking early in her career as a librarian. She is currently involved in projects such as establishing a monographic data base for OCLC and continuing education for network members. As Commissioner of CONTU, she has published a book entitled *New Technological Uses of Copyrighted Works,* under the sponsorship of President Carter.

ACRONYMS

AACR — Anglo-American Cataloging Rules
ABA — American Bar Association
ABS — Abstracts
ALA — American Library Association
BALLOTS — Bibliographic Automation of Large Library Operations Using a Time-Sharing System
BIOSIS — Bio-Science Information Service
BRS — Bibliographic Retrieval Services
CA — Chemical Abstracts
CAO — County Administrator's Office
CAPCON — Capitol Consortia Network
CDLC — Capital District Library Council
CLA — California Library Association
CLR — Council on Library Resources
COM — Computer Output Microfilm
CONSER — Conversion of Serials Project
CPS — Characters Per Second
CRT — Cathode Ray Tube
DDC — Defense Documentation Center
DE — Descriptor
DOS — Disk Operating System
ERIC — Educational Resources Information Center
FAUL — Five Associated University Libraries
FCC — Federal Communications Commission
FEDLINK — Federal Library Network
FOB — Free on Board
FTE — Full-Time Equivalent
ILLINET — Illinois Library Network
INCOLSA — Indiana Cooperative Library Services Authority
INFORM — International Reference Organization in Forensic Medicine and Sciences
INSPEC — Information Service in Physics, Electrotechnology and Control
ISAM — Indexed Sequential Access Method
ISBD — International Standard Bibliographic Description
ISBD-M — International Standard Bibliographic Description-Monographs
ISBD-S — International Standard Bibliographic Description-Serials
ISSN — International Standard Serial Number

LC — Library of Congress
LSCA — Library Services and Construction Act
MARC — Machine-Readable Cataloging
MARC-S — Machine-Readable Cataloging-Serials
MEDLARS — Medical Literature Analysis and Retrieval System
MHECB — Minnesota Higher Education Coordinating Board
MIDLNET — Midwest Regional Library Network
MINITEX — Minnesota Interlibrary Telecommunications Exchange
MLC — Medical Library Center
MULS — Minnesota Union List of Serials
NASA — National Aeronautics and Space Administration
NASIC — Northeast Academic Science Information Center
NDULS — North Dakota Union List of Serials
NEH — National Endowment for the Humanities
NELINET — New England Library and Information Network
NLM — National Library of Medicine
NTIS — National Technical Information Service
NUC — National Union Catalog
OCLC — Ohio College Library Center
OS — Operating System
PALINET — Pennsylvania Automated Library Network
PRLC — Pittsburgh Regional Library Center
RCA — Radio Corporation of America
SDC — System Development Corporation
SOLINET — Southeastern Library Network
SUNY — State University of New York
UCC — Uniform Commercial Code
UCSD — University of California at San Diego
ULMS — Union List of Montana Serials
VSAM — Virtual Storage Access Method

INDEX